LIVING THE QUESTIONS OF THE BIBLE

WORSHIP AND WITNESS

The Worship and Witness series seeks to foster a rich, interdisciplinary conversation on the theology and practice of public worship, a conversation that will be integrative and expansive. Integrative, in that scholars and practitioners from a wide range of disciplines and ecclesial contexts will contribute studies that engage church and academy. Expansive, in that the series will engage voices from the global church and foreground crucial areas of inquiry for the vitality of public worship in the twenty-first century.

The Worship and Witness series demonstrates and cultivates the interaction of topics in worship studies with a range of crucial questions, topics, and insights drawn from other fields. These include the traditional disciplines of theology, history, and pastoral ministry—as well as cultural studies, political theology, spirituality, and music and the arts. The series focus will thus bridge church worship practices and the vital witness these practices nourish.

We are pleased that you have chosen to join us in this conversation, and we look forward to sharing this learning journey with you.

Series Editors:
John D. Witvliet
Noel Snyder
Maria Cornou

LIVING THE QUESTIONS OF THE BIBLE

Luke A. Powery

CASCADE *Books* • Eugene, Oregon

LIVING THE QUESTIONS OF THE BIBLE

Worship and Witness

Cascade Books
An Imprint of Wipf and Stock Publishers
199 W. 8th Ave., Suite 3
Eugene, OR 97401

www.wipfandstock.com

PAPERBACK ISBN: 978-1-7252-5837-2
HARDCOVER ISBN: 978-1-7252-5838-9
EBOOK ISBN: 978-1-7252-5839-6

Cataloguing-in-Publication data:

Names: Powery, Luke A., author.

Title: Living the questions of the Bible / Luke A. Powery.

Description: Eugene, OR: Cascade Books, 2023 | Series: Worship and Witness | Includes bibliographical references.

Identifiers: ISBN 978-1-7252-5837-2 (paperback) | ISBN 978-1-7252-5838-9 (hardcover) | ISBN 978-1-7252-5839-6 (ebook)

Subjects: LCSH: Bible—Hermeneutics. | Spirituality.

Classification: BT1103 P665 2023 (paperback) | BT1103 (ebook)

05/12/23

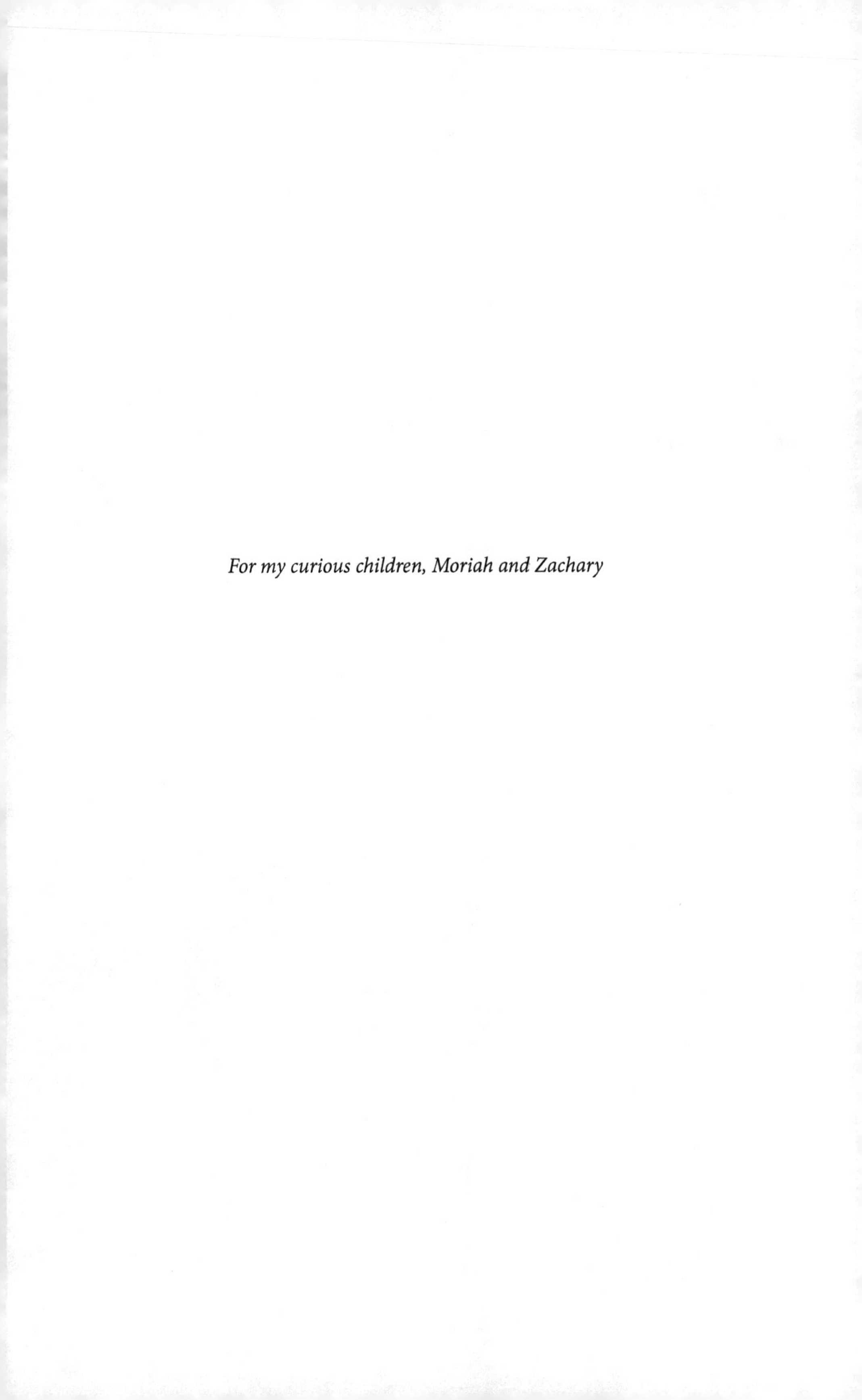

For my curious children, Moriah and Zachary

Contents

Acknowledgments

Over twenty years ago, I was ordained at Union Baptist Church on Pennington Avenue in Trenton, New Jersey, and what a journey it has been. Preaching, teaching, writing, singing, leading. When Jesus said, "Come and see" to me, I never imagined seeing and experiencing such a holy adventure. But what I've realized the most on this path is that I've never been alone. Of course, God has been with me because God is a "with" God, but so have a cloud of witnesses on earth as it is in heaven. People don't have to be "with" you; they can choose to be "against" you. But when I look back over my life and think things over, I can truly say that I've been blessed, and my testimony is that many have been "with" me through varied circumstances of life. For this realization, I give thanks. As my father would say, "Thank ya!"

There are so many witnesses to whom to say "thank ya"—for their encouragement, belief in me, guidance, prayers, truth-telling, creative energy, friendship, mutual laughter, and so much more. I've been touched by so many thus this book of reflections has been touched implicitly by these faithful witnesses all over the world. When someone asks me how long it takes to prepare a sermon, my answer is always, "My whole life." This book is no different. It has taken a whole life, my whole life, to write this book.

This book would not have been written without the sabbatical given to me by Duke president Vincent Price in the spring of 2020. I'm grateful to him and Duke University for the academic privilege of having a sabbatical where I could focus on this project, uninterrupted by administrative work. Heartfelt thanks are also due to my colleagues at Duke Chapel, especially Amanda Hughes and Bruce Puckett, who willingly took on more leadership responsibilities at the chapel during my sabbatical, as well as my assistant, Ava West, who keeps me organized and ably handled logistical and administrative matters related to this book project. Also, I'm grateful to the Duke Chapel community as a whole because they understand when a leader needs a sabbatical and extend grace for it to happen and to continue even when a global pandemic hits. Beyond Duke, there are seminaries, divinity schools, and churches who invited me for lectureships and talks where these ideas were disseminated, and questions raised by audiences. Those questions led me to believe that we do live the questions of the Bible and that a book like this one would be welcome in the church writ large. I'm thankful that those learning communities had hospitable ears.

Furthermore, in my work as a professor, former students at Princeton Theological Seminary and Duke Divinity School pressed me and the Bible with questions, some of which have no answers. I'm grateful for these students for raising questions in the classroom that may have never been safe enough to utter anywhere else.

At any institution, if you have a gifted research and teaching assistant, then it is a grace. Peace Lee was that embodied grace as a phenomenal research and teaching assistant. She provided research for writing and sermons and sparked ongoing inspirational dialogue while TA'ing my Howard Thurman class. I'm thankful that Peace asks incredible questions.

Moreover, one question led to this book—"What are you thinking about writing next?" It came from editor Michael Thomson when he was with Eerdmans, but that question brought me back to him in his new home at Wipf and Stock. To make a book happen, there's always the gift of an editor who believes in you and your work, so I'm grateful to Michael for his encouragement in this endeavor and to the imprint of Cascade Books for taking it on.

Thanks is also due to Wipf and Stock for giving permission to republish two sermons from *Preaching Prophetic Care* under different titles—"What does this mean?" and "Where have they come from?"—and to Abingdon Press for giving permission to republish one sermon from *The Abingdon Preaching Annual 2018*—"Why are you weeping?"

This supportive cloud of witnesses is made more whole when I turn to my family. I give thanks to my parents, the Rev. W. Byron Powery, and Emittie Powery, who gave me a respect and love for Scripture. I express bountiful gratitude to my wife, Gail, and my children, Moriah and Zachary—to whom this book is dedicated—for the space and time they give me to do my best work and for their faith that inspires me in my ongoing quest with God. Gospel singer and composer Andrae Crouch summed it up best with his own question: "How can I say thanks for all the things you have done for me?"

Prelude

The Bible, Questions, and the Life of Faith

"Why are you afraid?" It was a question Jesus asked his disciples in a boat after calming a storm (Mark 4). But it was also a question that I used for a sermon title when interviewing for my current job at Duke University. "Why are you afraid?" As I walked into the pulpit on that Sunday morning in June 2012, it hit me—that question of Jesus used as my sermon title was a question from God to me. "Why are you afraid?" It was an unexpected professional opportunity with lots of unknowns, and to be honest, I was afraid of what was to come and what God might be doing. I had lots of questions, and truthfully, we, Christians, have lots of questions as disciples of Jesus.

I thought that probing interrogation from Jesus to his disciples in the boat was a question for the congregation before me and perhaps it was, but in that unfamiliar neo-Gothic setting of Duke Chapel, it was also a question to me. "Why are you afraid?" It was another experience in my life of faith where I learned how often we have and live questions, not answers, how often God questions us or uses Scripture to probe us, such that literal biblical questions like the one in the Gospel of Mark from the mouth of Jesus, become our own spiritual investigation of our soul. On that Sunday morning, that was Jesus's question to me. It was one of those moments when I was preaching to myself.

An ancient question was still a contemporary one, a very human query. So often the Bible is presented as an answer book, as if it has all the answers to all of our questions, as if the life of faith is only about answers. But what I've been reminded of over the last several years is that the Bible is also a question book, and the life of faith includes questions. From Genesis to Revelation, from the beginning to the end, questions are raised. The first question in the Bible is from the serpent to the woman in Genesis—"Did

God say, 'You shall not eat from any tree in the garden'?" (Gen 3:1). The last question in the Bible is raised by "all shipmasters and seafarers, sailors and all whose trade is on the sea" as Babylon falls—"What city was like the great city?" (Rev 18:17–18). Christian faith involves questions and faith is actually a quest. What would change if we saw the Bible as a question book, probing human life, querying God and through which God questions us? What if we embraced questioning as a vital part of faith and discipleship? After all, the Bible doesn't just have answers; it has questions, literally. And these questions point us to living in the unresolved, the unknown, the unchartered roads, the unmarked alleyways. Scripture leads us to live the questions and embrace an interrogative spirituality.

Remember, "having right answers does not mean one knows God."[1] Perhaps we find God in the questions, a God who even asks questions, as this book will reveal. One of my mentors, the late Vanderbilt University professor Dale Andrews, was known to have this mantra: "I have more questions than answers, more problems than solutions. For this, I give God praise." What does it mean to give God praise for more questions than answers? What does it mean to thank God for inhabiting the realm of disequilibrium? This is an honest acknowledgement of the truth and the freedom that comes from abiding in the truth of uncertainty and incomprehensibility, rather than trying to inhabit cities of certainty that will one day crumble and fall like Babylon. "I have more questions than answers." Isn't that the truth of Christian discipleship?

In *Letters to a Young Poet,* Rainer Maria Rilke wrote this to his nineteen-year-old protégé:

> . . . be patient toward all that is unsolved in your heart and to try to *love the questions themselves* like locked rooms and like books that are written in a very foreign tongue. Do not now seek the answers, which cannot be given you because you would not be able to live them. And the point is, to live everything. *Live the questions* now. Perhaps you will then gradually, without noticing it, live along some distant day into the answer.[2]

The Bible is a question book. It has its own questions for us, to us, about us. We don't have to make up questions; they are right there in God's Word. There are many human questions from the divine word. It's as if God's Word speaks our language, knows our hearts, discerns our struggles, and asks our questions. God's Word includes questioning from the mouth of God and human beings. Questions like: Where are you? Who told you that you were

1. Craddock, *Luke*, 150.
2. Rilke, *Letters to a Young Poet.*

naked? Why did it yield wild grapes? Why have you forsaken me? Who will separate us from the love of Christ? Who is worthy to open the scroll? Why do we fast, but you do not see? Is there no balm in Gilead? Why are you afraid? How can this be since I am a virgin? Will he find faith on earth? Why are you weeping? How can I sing a song in a strange land? Which commandment is the first of all? And who is my neighbor? Where have they come from? These are examples of the various questions straight out of the Bible for the life of faith, demonstrating that we should live everything, including the questions. William O'Daly writes in his Introduction to his translation of Pablo Neruda's *Book of Questions:* "Our greatest act of faith" may be "living in a state of visionary surrender to the elemental questions, free of the quiet desperation of clinging too tightly to answers."[3]

This may not only be true in relation to the Bible, but it may also be true for how we view Jesus. Sometimes, I wonder if we make Jesus not only a Santa Claus, giving us everything we ask for, but a security blanket that squeezes out any kind of mystery in the life of faith, making it more scientific logic than artful, exploratory love. "Jesus is the answer for the world today, above him there's no other, Jesus is the way," the song says. On one level, I understand this as a Christian, but on another level, this phraseology—Jesus is the answer—may short-circuit conversations and not allow for deeper questioning and exploration in the life of faith. Jesus is not only the answer, but Jesus is the eternal incarnate question of God to the world—"Do you love me?" (John 21). Jesus asks questions like that one and the one raised to his disciples in the boat. Jesus is the question because when we encounter him in a boat or boardroom, when we meet God's presence in the Spirit, there are questions raised. "Who do you say that I am"? Jesus asked Peter when they encountered each other (Matt 15:16). When we encounter Jesus, there will be questions from us and to us.

Jesus is the question about our way of life—Who am I really? Who am I supposed to be? What am I doing with my life? What shall I cry? Where am I going? What is the meaning of life? Questions are open-ended, meaning they are eternal, and we will continue to inhabit them as we follow Jesus. In his presence, our lives are illuminated, questioned, and we begin our own self-interrogation as we look at ourselves in the light of Christ. Jesus is the question, the quest, the way; and, "the quest [is] the destination"[4] for us. Like Howard Thurman, we are challenged to pursue the quest with questioning and see this as an act of faithfulness. One cannot face Jesus and not pause to ponder and wonder and even doubt, for a little bit.

3. Smith, "Conclusion," 174.

4. Smith, "Conclusion," 173.

This querying approach may make some uneasy, but it is a biblical approach to the life of faith, and it indicates that we know that we do not have all the answers. Quoting Bible verses does not give all the answers nor erase the questions we may have, especially when the Bible is full of actual questions. To question as a pathway of Christian faithfulness suggests a sense of humility, both intellectual and spiritual. It also reveals a spiritual searching. Remember, the motto of St. Anselm of Canterbury was "faith seeking understanding." It is not that we will always understand but that we seek, which is critical for faith. Seeking is vital and that is what questioning is as it keeps the possibilities open, inflecting toward the truth. It is not about arrival but about the process, the quest, the Way, following Jesus, questioning Jesus while being questioned ourselves.

The purpose of this book of reflections is to follow the pattern and language of Scripture by reminding Christians that questions are also the mother tongue of faith. Thus, this is a question book not an answer book. It aims to affirm an interrogative spirituality as a faithful Christian practice. So often as adults we lose the curiosity of our childhood, closing off mystery and joyful expectation. All we want are answers and at times we demand them, becoming frustrated with ambiguity and openness.

My children, to whom this book is dedicated, never ceased to raise questions when they were younger. One day, I was driving my car with my son, Zachary, who was eight years old at the time, sitting in the backseat. Driving with your child provides ample time to talk about all sorts of things. Disney Infinity characters. The Miami Heat basketball team. His behavior at school. Sleeping through my sermons. The little girls he thought were disgusting for hugging him. Life and death. On this particular car ride, Zachary asked me, "Dad, are you going to heaven?" I paused and thought, "I need to get this right." I said, "That's my hope." He responded confidently, "You're going, because you pray, you're the dean, and you do good stuff." He was curious about the heaven he heard about in the Bible, and he wanted me to be sure I would one day be a citizen of it.

My daughter, Moriah, was no different at the young age of three years old. One evening, I sat down at the dinner table while Moriah was waiting for me at the table. Her mother told me that Moriah had a question for me about Good Friday and she wanted to wait for me to get home to ask it. I thought "cool, my daughter is curious liturgically and theologically." Moriah's question was this: "What is Good Friday?" I started explaining the significance of the day and speaking of the crucifixion of Jesus and she stopped me in my tracks and declared, "That's no fun!" She was so right. Good Friday isn't "fun." But it's real and honest, just like questions of faith or about faith.

Questions are not antithetical to following Jesus and my children exemplified this early on. Questions are included as a part of faith, just as the language of the Bible reveals. One believes God but can still ask God questions. The truth is that even as Christians we don't know everything about God, the church, or faith. An example of this is Acts 19. In that story, some disciples from Ephesus come to Paul and say they hadn't even heard of the Holy Spirit, so he lays hands on them to receive the Spirit. When he does, the Spirit comes upon them, they speak in tongues and prophesy, that is, there is the gift of both incomprehensibility (tongues) and comprehensibility (prophesying). Disciples didn't know everything and even when they receive the Spirit, there is still incomprehension. This is why we keep asking questions in life before God. What this book aims to do is to show how faith as expressed in the Bible includes questions, hopefully freeing us to do the same today.

This book is organized in three sections that are centered on three questions. The first section is "Who Is God?" and offers reflections from various portions of Scripture on specific questions from the biblical text. Those particular questions foster further thinking related to the larger umbrella question about who God is. In general, this first section is focused on God's identity and who God is and what God is about and what questions God may even ask. The second section is "Who Am I?" and offers reflections from various parts of Scripture on specific questions from the biblical text as well. These questions aim to help the reader ponder more deeply about human identity and who we are and what questions we ask in the life of faith. The final and third section is "What Should We Do?," and like the other sections offers reflections on questions from particular Bible passages as a way to help the reader reflect on how we should live in the world as people of faith in light of who God is and who we are.

One might notice that there is overlap at times with the various questions across the sections, meaning that there is not always a clear demarcation between the questions God asks and the ones we raise. I say this because God's questions are sometimes our own and our questions can also be found in the mouth of God. This isn't surprising per se, because God in Jesus Christ is both divine and human, and so are the questions. Also, at the end of each reflection there are some "questions about the question" for further reflection as an individual or in smaller group settings. The goal is not to arrive at answers per se but to keep asking questions and keep the conversation (*homiletos*) going, because in the questioning, we may find God right there, asking us questions too. All of this may lead to new depths of spiritual discovery; as the famous medical researcher Jonas Salk once said, "What people think of as the moment of discovery is really the discovery of the question."[5]

I hope the reader finds that discovering the question can also be the discovery of a holy life with a holy God. When Job questions his horrific suffering and plight and grapples with his human condition, even as a "blameless and upright" (Job 1:1) man, God eventually responds to him out of a whirlwind. And how does God respond? With questions. "Who is this that darkens counsel by words without knowledge? . . . Where were you when I laid the foundation of the earth?" (Job 38:2, 6). Job is not reprimanded for having questions and concerns, and why would he be when this is how God responds in this situation? If you follow God's way, you will have questions. May this book give you more questions to live than answers to give. Live the questions, ancient and contemporary, and love the questions because this will help you become more like God.

5. *Jonas Salk Quotes.*

1

WHO IS GOD?

1

Why did it yield wild grapes?

(Isa 5:1–7)

There was a middle-aged woman who had a heart attack and she was taken to the hospital. While on the operating table, she had a near-death experience. During that experience, she saw God and asked if this was it. God said "No" and explained that she had another thirty to forty years to live. Upon her recovery, she decided to just stay in the hospital and have a face lift, liposuction, breast augmentation, and a tummy tuck. She even had someone come in and change her hair color. She figured that since she had another thirty or forty years she might as well make the most of it. But when she walked out of the hospital after her last operation, she was hit and killed by an ambulance speeding up to the hospital. She arrived in front of God and asked, "I thought you said I had another thirty to forty years?" God replied, "Sorry, I didn't recognize you."[1]

What we expect is not always what we get. You don't have to live that long to figure this out. I don't even recognize the prophet Isaiah. The Old Testament prophet-preacher, Isaiah, surprised me. I was expecting him to preach in his usual way. I expected his sermon to be the same old story with the same old tune, since some preachers only have one good sermon. I was expecting Isaiah to rant and rave and rain down doom and gloom on us, which might work for ministers who specialize in abusing the people in the pew. Isaiah would be a great preacher in that kind of congregation because

1. Murphy, "Afterlife is a prime subject for humor."

there's so much trouble in his sermons without any signs of grace. Lots of bad news, little good news. Do you know any preachers like that?

I expected Isaiah to preach what he preaches many Sundays after the choir anthem. Have you ever heard Isaiah preach? Like when he said, "Ah, sinful nation, people laden with iniquity, offspring who do evil, children who deal corruptly, who have forsaken the Lord, who have despised the Holy One of Israel, who are utterly estranged! Why do you seek further beatings? Why do you continue to rebel? The whole head is sick and the whole heart faint . . . How the faithful city has become a whore! The Lord will afflict with scabs the heads of the daughters of Zion." What a sermon! How would you like to be a member at The Trouble-On-Every-Side Temple of Isaiah? No wonder his church membership is declining. If only he would melodiously preach like he does in this passage, his members might return.

Isaiah surprised me. Something got a hold of him. When I was expecting the prophet Isaiah to preach the terrors, damning us right into hell Jonathan Edwards style, he didn't do it. Instead, he sang a warm sermonic love song about his beloved God, Luther Vandross style—"Here and now, I promise to love faithfully." I never expected him to sing a sermon like that. There are singing preachers, but Isaiah? He surprised me. But what we expect is not always what we get.

Isaiah's sermon tune is different because he's in love and love will make you do things you don't normally do. Love will make you go cuckoo for Cocoa Puffs! Love will make your toes get tingly, knees wobbly, skin sweaty, eyes blurry so you can't see straight. And now, I know it can even make you preach better. We say love is blind, but Isaiah sees his beloved and the situation crisp and clear. Prophet Isaiah can't help but croon a beautiful ballad for God, his beloved. He's in love. But this song is not just about God but God's vineyard. These words are potent with lovely poetry and a hopeful expectation of the harvest due to the care God gives the vineyard. And when God does something, God does it right.

God's vineyard is in a fertile place on a hill; the soil is ripe for producing juicy grapes. The setting is perfect, and if that isn't enough, the Lord's preparation is executed according to the rules of agriculture. God digs the soil and clears it of stones. Then God plants choice vines—the best of the best, the crème de la crème. God invests blood, sweat, and tears into this vineyard, but most of all, God invests divine love. Homeland Security should talk to God because the beloved God even builds a watchtower in the middle of the vineyard in order to protect it from intruders or predators who might destroy this natural work of art. Love will make you want to protect your loved ones. And if that isn't enough, God creates a wine vat to prepare for the sweet wine that is expected to come so that it can be shared with others.

God does everything perfectly. God does everything by the book. God does all that God can and Isaiah keeps singing his heart out.

He sings at this point in ecstasy, as his voice and soul are filled with love for God and great expectations. His voice crescendos to the anticipated climax in volume and energy, as we, the listeners, await the inevitable—the yielding of grapes. For even the beloved, God, expected the vineyard to yield grapes. Based on God's financial investment and physical and emotional efforts, God expects the best from the vineyard. Who wouldn't after all of that?

We expect the best from our children as we raise them and pour our lives into them. We expect the best from our spouses as we do the best we can and love them until death do us part. We expect the best from our friends in whom we've confided our secrets. We expect the best from our boyfriends or girlfriends after all that money we've spent on each other. We expect the best from our schools and professors after dutifully paying tuition. We expect the best from our employers after working extra time for no extra pay. We expect the best from our doctors' health advice. We expect the best from our pastors, religious leaders, and politicians. We expect the best from our financial advisers. But if you live long enough, you'll discover that you can expect the best all you want and still get the worst, because what we expect is not always what we get.

Isaiah discovers this truth as he sings his sermon for God because his ballad soon experiences a mood swing. As we expect this lost-in-love singing preacher to reach the climax in volume and energy to the yielding of grapes, we unexpectedly experience a key change from major to minor, from hopefulness to hopelessness, from delight to despair, from sweet expectations to bitter disappointment. One might think this song is no longer about love, but it is! Because as philosopher Nicholas Wolterstorff reminds us, "every lament is a love song."[2] Lamenting what could have been or should have been. Lamenting lost hopes and dreams. Isaiah is singing the blues. At this juncture, this song of lament is about love gone wrong, something about which we all know too well as we hear of the statistics of domestic violence and sexual harassment. Love gone wrong. We don't need to watch soap operas like *All My Children*, *General Hospital*, or even *As the World Turns*. We know how the world turns.

We're living in the chaos ourselves and it's turning us upside down, inside out. Our lives are soap operas, making us testify like poet Langston Hughes and say that "life for me ain't been no crystal stair."[3] We have our

2. Wolterstorff, *Lament for a Son*, 6.

3. Hughes, "Mother to Son."

very own soap opera right here in Scripture. Forget about Chris Brown, Rihanna, Kanye West, and Kim Kardashian. Read the news flash about God. God "expected [the vineyard] to yield grapes but it yielded wild grapes." Love gone wrong. Unrequited love. Unmet expectations. The sorrowful divine beloved even questions, "When I expected it to yield grapes, why did it yield wild grapes?" All of the intensive labor of love for the harvest was lost. All of that effort for nothing. All of that money for nothing. All of that time for nothing. All of that sacrifice for nothing. All of those late nights for nothing. All of those prayers for nothing. All of those tears for nothing. Unmet expectations.

The wealthiest country in the world, the United States of America, a nation that can spend trillions of dollars on war, cannot find enough money to aid dilapidated schools in urban areas and provide adequate educational resources for children of color?! No child left behind? Children are being left behind and many are being put behind bars in a disproportionate manner. Expecting justice but seeing more bloodshed. "When I expected it to yield grapes, why did it yield wild grapes?"

The church used to be a place of refuge from violence. These days rage can happen right on the doorsteps of the church or inside of it. Several years ago, outside a Baptist church, a man fatally shot his estranged wife in the church parking lot while their daughter worshipped inside the sanctuary. And, look at what happened at Mother Emmanuel AME church in Charleston, South Carolina, in June 2015. "When I expected it to yield grapes, why did it yield wild grapes?"

It seems as if violence is winning the victory. Young black men playing in parks, walking home with iced tea and Skittles, driving home or to work or to the movies, end up getting shot by police officers. "When I expected it to yield grapes, why did it yield wild grapes?"

In August 2017, Hurricane Harvey created a modern-day hell for so many. Officer Steve Perez left his home to help those in need during the storm. His wife asked him not to go but the dedicated, determined, daring Perez told her, "We've got work to do." On his way to work that Sunday, he drowned. "When I expected it to yield grapes, why did it yield wild grapes?"

I still remember Sis Jean. She had a big smile on her face and a bounce in her step every Sunday. We sang in the choir together when I was a teenager. I can still hear her greeting me—"Hi, Bro. Luke." She had a way of saying it—"Bro. Luke." After several years passed, I visited my home in Miami, Florida, expecting to hear good news about the sweet elder Christian sisters from my youth. Instead, I found out that the bounce in Sis Jean's step had been stolen. Stolen by a sickness that was decaying her body. She still went to church. She even had special seating—a couch right in the front of the church. They put it there so she could still hear the songs of Zion. They put it there so she could rest when needed. Her heart still sang even though it was broken. Broken because the disease she had was AIDS, contracted from her very own husband who had been fooling around. A God-fearing, churchgoing woman with AIDS. "When I expected it to yield grapes, why did it yield wild grapes?"

Unmet expectations—in the world, in this country, in the broader society, in your community, in your church, in your marriage, in your relationships, in your families, at your jobs, at your schools, in your Christian journey. Things aren't the way you thought they would be or should be. One day you're healthy, the next day you find out you have cancer. One day you're planning your family vacation, the next day your spouse says he or she is leaving you for someone else. One day you're up, the next day you're down. One day you're to the left, the next day your only option is to go right. In other words, when I expected apples, how did I end up with oranges? When I ordered a hot cordon bleu, why did I end up with frozen chicken nuggets? Life can get wild and go out of control sometimes with all of the twists and turns, ups and downs. Receiving something you never ordered in life. So you may find yourself lying in your bed at night, crying yourself to sleep in a pool of tears, "When I expected it to yield grapes, why did it yield wild grapes?"

The circumstances of life teach us to expect the unexpected, the wild grapes. But when life yields wild grapes, it's not easy to digest. God even asks, "What more was there to do for my vineyard that I have not done in it?" "I've done all that I can!" Almighty God is at God's wit's end! And what happens next could happen to anyone of us. Unmet expectations can lead to destruction. God decides to destroy the fruitless vineyard, which is Israel, and allows it to go into exile (5:13). At times, we may even ask, "What more could I have done?" or "What did I do wrong?," which can lead to self-blame and pity, causing us to become disillusioned with God and life. We, too, then may go into a type of exile, isolation, and disconnection from others and God, feeling hopeless. The worst-case scenario would be that we destroy ourselves, spiritual suicide, or others, spiritual homicide. "How can I sing the Lord's song in this strange land of the unexpected?" "My God, my God, why have you forsaken me?"(Ps 22). Jesus, the vine, even experienced a wooden exile. How can I trust you, God, when all that my life bears are wild grapes?

The answer to that question is also in the mouth of the singing prophet-preacher Isaiah, but in his later sermons. This lamenting love song sermon is not the whole story of love. No one sermon can tell it all. Love has its ups and love has its downs. Even the cross of Christ alone is not the entire gospel story. There are times when you can't just preach the text because we're called to preach the gospel, however, the biblical text is a window to the gospel. This means you've got to tell the whole gospel story. You've got to know the whole gospel story. You can't just preach a little portion of Scripture and assume that will provide good news and hope. You can't just read chapter 5 and not know what happens in chapter 40. You can't just show a three-minute YouTube clip and think that is the sum of a person or a sermon. You can't just analyze the beginning and neglect the ending because the ending in fact is our starting point. The end is the beginning for us. The end will be our spiritual compass.

In the end of this story, Israel's expectations are not met because their expectations are too low. In the end of this story, we realize that what we expect is not always what we get. We might have thought this was just another story of love gone wrong. We might have thought that God was like everyone else. But the Holy One is not just anyone.

Isaiah's sermonic corpus has other songs that we should know about. This singing preacher not only sings himself, but preaches of a day when Israel, herself, will sing of the goodness of the Lord. They will have a song in the night (30:29) and eventually they will sing a new song (42:10). The old thing becomes a thing that is new. The weariness of the wilderness becomes a wilderness full of water. A rancid desert becomes a desert with rivers. A pouting party becomes a party of praise. Israel will have a reason to sing! And we will have a reason to sing. The minor melody of the song of the vineyard is not the end of this love story for though Israel experiences exile, their tune eventually modulates back to a major key because God delivers them and brings them to their own land (chapter 14). Isaiah sings about their future of thanksgiving and comfort and salvation and trust and joy (chapter 12). The sorrowful song of the vineyard is only one part of this sacred oratorio because in the end, God is faithful to God's people. It's simple but so true. The end of the story should actually be our beginning. The end should be our starting point as we view life—God's faithfulness. God's covenantal love that never lets us go. That should be our life's presupposition, our life's hermeneutic, the lens through which we view the world—God is faithful.

Just ask the children of Israel, who expected to be in slavery their whole life, but God raised up Moses to tell Pharaoh "Let my people go!" Just ask Abraham, who expected to sacrifice his only son on an altar, but God sent a CNN news flash through an angel to tell him "don't lay your hand on the boy" because God had a ram in the bush. Just ask Job, who had everything and lost everything and expected to finally lose his life, but God restored his fortunes and gave him twice as much as he had before. Just ask the psalmist, who expected to be destroyed by flying arrows in the day and pestilence at night, but God gave him refuge and shelter in the shadow of divine wings. Just ask Isaiah, who knew that the youth expected to faint and fall exhausted, but God sent a word saying, "Those who wait for the Lord shall renew their strength, they shall mount up with wings like eagles, they shall run and not be weary, they shall walk and not faint." Just ask Mary, a young virgin girl, who expected to live just an ordinary life on the fringes of society as an outcast good-for-nothing woman, but God chose her womb to enter the world as the Savior of humanity. Just ask the crazy Gerasene demoniac who expected to stay out of his mind, but Jesus touched him, clothed him in his right mind, and made him a preacher. Just ask Jesus, who went from divinity to humanity, who was high but stooped low, "who was conceived by the Holy Ghost, born of the virgin Mary, suffered under Pontius Pilate, was crucified, dead, and buried; and descended into hell." Just ask Jesus, who many expected never to see again, but the Apostles' Creed declares, on "The third day He arose again from the dead; He ascended into heaven, and sitteth on the right hand of God the Father Almighty; from thence he shall come to judge the quick and the dead." Maybe not in the beginning, maybe not even right now, but in the end, you will know that God is faithful to God's people. Weeping may endure for the night, but joy comes in the morning.

God will not meet our expectations. God will magnify them. God will do exceedingly abundantly above all we ask or even imagine. "When you pass through the waters, I will be with you and through the rivers, they shall not overwhelm you; when you walk through fire you shall not be burned, and the flame shall not consume you. For I am the Lord your God, the Holy One of Israel, your Savior, you're precious in my sight and I love you." What a love song! We might have expected God to be like everyone but the Holy One is not just anyone.

God is faithful. Unmet expectations, wild grapes, are a fact of life, but they do not tell the end of the story. God does. We may not always get what we expect, but we can always expect God to be faithful. Or, as a friend of mine once said, "A setback is just a setup for a comeback."

Questions about the Question

- When in your life have you experienced unmet expectations?
- What have you learned when your expectations have not been met?
- What expectations do you have of God?

2

What do you want me to do for you?

(Mark 10:35–52)

What have you to do with us? Have you come to destroy us? What is this? Why does this fellow speak in this way? Who can forgive sins but God alone? Why does he eat with tax collectors and sinners? Why do John's disciples and the disciples of the Pharisees fast, but your disciples do not fast? Why are they doing what is not lawful on the Sabbath? Do you not care that we are perishing? Who then is this that even the wind and sea obey him? What have you to do with me, Son of the Most High God? Where did this man get all of this? What is this wisdom that has been given to him? Is not this the carpenter? Why do your disciples not live according to the tradition of the elders? How can one feed these people with bread here in the desert? Why could we not cast it out? Is it lawful for a man to divorce his wife? What must I do to inherit eternal life? Who can be saved? These are questions people ask Jesus throughout the Gospel of Mark. We tend to ask Jesus lots of questions, sometimes almost putting him on trial in the courtroom where we are judge and jury. Questioning God can be a way of engaging God and leaning into God's presence with deep trust and curiosity. It doesn't have to be combative or coercive. Questioning can be a form of genuine caring. You ask Jesus because you care.

The same is true for Jesus. He cares so much about us that he has his own questions for us. "Why do you raise such questions in your heart? Who do you say that I am?" In this Gospel lesson, he asks the disciples, "What do you want me to do for you?" Jesus asks that question after James and John tell him that they want him to do whatever they ask him to do. Sounds like a good deal to them, making Jesus a cosmic bellhop. Their answer to his question is that one of them wants to sit at his right hand and the other on his left, in his glory. They don't really know for what they are asking. They can't discern the difference between wants and needs. They want glory but demonstrate they have no clue what that really is. Jesus just predicted his death and resurrection for the third time, and they are already considering their place in the new holy administration. They were lobbying for cabinet positions even while Jesus was beginning his funeral procession toward Jerusalem. The disciples dream about palatial banquets celebrating Christ's coronation, but what they don't know at this point is that they will eventually find two criminals on crosses with Jesus, "one on his right and one on his left" (15:27). That's where God's glory will take you—to a cross. The disciples ask for something they don't even understand.

People want glory, honor, power, wealth, and riches, but even many of the rich and famous know that they are not the answer to a life of contentment. We ought to be careful what we ask for; we may actually receive it. As actor Denzel Washington has said, "You pray for rain, you gotta deal with the mud too."[1] If you ask for a crown, there will also be a cross because there are no resurrections without crucifixions. The pursuit of power is a manifestation of a present weakness. If you want glory, in the Christian life, it is gory. If you find yourself desiring to be on top, it may be like the top of a pyramid where you are all alone by yourself—at the top but terribly lonely. There may be a price to pay for what you pray.

Before you jump on the bandwagon of thinking Jesus will do whatever you want and you can pull a slot machine of spiritual power and a utopian blessing will pour out, you should keep in mind that Jesus asks this same question to blind Bartimaeus after Jesus speaks with James and John. "What do you want me to do for you?" Bartimaeus responds, "Teacher, let me see again." The irony is that Bartimaeus's answer should have been the disciples' response. "Let me see again." Bartimaeus requested a need and the disciples, though they were not physically blind, were spiritually blind. They don't really know what they need; they need to have their eyes open to their real needs and ask for it—"let me see again."

This is true for us many times when we don't even know what to pray or how to pray. We yearn to speak to God but maybe we have no idea where to really begin and how to articulate the sighs of our hearts with our stammering tongues. Maybe we should just pray, "Let me see again." Let me see what I really need in my life. Let me see what I should really be doing in

1. Washington, *Goodreads Quotes*.

the world. Let me see what glory really is. Let me see the cost of glory and power before I start asking for it. Let me see how my life costs you your life. Our prayer should be the Bartimaeus petition—"let me see again." Let me recognize that your glory manifests in selfless service, in dying to help others live and that to be great is to serve, to be great is to love, to be great is to do justice, love kindness, and walk humbly with God. "Whoever wishes to be great among you must be your servant."

In a sermon titled "The Drum Major Instinct," Dr. Martin Luther King Jr. preaches this: greatness "means that everybody can be great because everybody can serve. You don't have to know about Plato and Aristotle to serve . . . You don't have to know the second law of thermodynamics to serve. You only need a heart full of grace, a soul generated by love."[2] Let me see Jesus that I may see what it means to serve. The greatness of God manifest in Jesus is gory glory on a criminal's cross and can even be seen wherever a basin and towel are made ready to wash dirty, stinky feet.

We have the different answers of the disciples and Bartimaeus to the question of Jesus and can affirm the truth that we may not always ask rightly or wisely, and we should, as a former seminary peer once said, "check ourselves before we wreck ourselves." Yet, we can't underestimate what Jesus will do when we respond to his question, "What do you want me to do for you?" It takes courage to truly ask for what we need. Perhaps we don't think God will answer, so we would rather not ask at all and build a steel wall of defense around our faith and heart. But as the song says, "If I never had a problem, I wouldn't know God could solve them."[3] Prayer, telling Jesus what you need, is not a magic wand and prayer doesn't change God; it changes you. Prayer doesn't change things, God does. And Jesus is asking that question to all of us: "What do you want me to do for you?" When you respond, you might be surprised by the answer you receive.

Someone talked about their experience with prayer and said this:

> I asked God for strength, that I might achieve,
> I was made weak, that I might learn humbly to obey.
> I asked for health, that I might do greater things,
> I was given infirmity, that I might do better things.
> I asked for riches, that I might be happy,
> I was given poverty, that I might be wise.
> I asked for power, that I might have the praise of [humans],
> I was given weakness, that I might feel the need of God. . . .
> I asked for all things, that I might enjoy life,

2. King, *The Drum Major Instinct*, 265–266.
3. Crouch, "Through It All."

I was given life, that I might enjoy all things.
I got nothing that I asked for—
But everything that I had hoped for . . .[4]

What is the one thing you want Jesus to do for you, the one thing you hope for but have been too timid to ask? Your answer may be what will help you see again as you wait for Jesus to act. If you never ask, you may never receive.

The question of Jesus is not only about us, probing our hearts and motivations; it also says something about God in Jesus Christ. "What do you want me to do for you?" It suggests that God wants to do something for you. Our misguided answers or unclear motivations don't stop Jesus from asking his heartfelt, personal question. He asks even if we answer in a distorted, unsure manner. He asks because of love. He asks because he cares. He asks because he wants to meet our needs, not that it is only about us in the Christian life. But today is your opportunity to answer his question, "What do you want me to do for you?" The good news is that Christ's faithfulness and activity is not predicated on our faithfulness or faithlessness. His faithfulness is predicated on the promises of God to be for us and with us till the end of the age.

That question from Jesus says something about God. How God desires to work on our behalf for our good. How God is a giving God. How God is willing to listen to our answers. How God is able to act and do for us. How God serves the world through the death and resurrection of Jesus Christ. God loves the world, but remember it includes you. God loves you. We may be more comfortable with a transcendent, distant deity who doesn't get involved in our affairs, but God loved the world so much that God became one of us in Jesus to be Emmanuel, "God with us." God's love leads God toward immanence and intimacy and interest in our particular lives and is as close as the breath flowing through our bodies. Thus, the question from Jesus shouldn't scare us but be a scriptural sign of how deeply he cares for us. He cares for you.

Jesus is dying to love us as a servant king, a servant leader, revealing how his power is to empower and serve others through his cruciform heart. Jesus gives without any strings attached. His love is so tender that his flesh is torn from his body for us. We may not have the answers we should, but Jesus still raises the question and his glory shines through it, as he's willing to serve and die for us. Jesus shows us how to find our lives by losing them for the sake of the people God loves so much.

"What do you want me to do for you?" This is also a question we should be asking one another because:

4. "Blessing of Unanswered Prayers."

If I can help somebody as I pass along,
If I can cheer somebody with a word or song,
If I can show somebody he's traveling wrong,
Then my living will not be in vain.
If I can do my duty as a Christian ought,
If I can bring salvation to a world once wrought,
If I can spread the message as the master taught,
Then my living will not be in vain.[5]

This is a question we should pose to each other but right now, Jesus is asking you, "What do you want me to do for you?" What will your answer be?

Questions about the Question

- How does this question from Jesus impact your understanding of God?
- If you could ask Jesus to do anything for you, what would it be?
- What hinders you from answering this question from Jesus?

5. Androzzo, "If I Can Help Somebody."

3

Do you think they were worse offenders?

(Luke 13:1–9)

If you live long enough, you'll realize that bad things happen to good people all the time. But when bad things happen to those deemed to be bad people, what do you think? How do you respond to "the Galileans whose blood Pilate had mingled with their sacrifices" or "those eighteen who were killed when the tower of Siloam fell on them"? Would we find rejoicing if we watched the media coverage of your heart? Did they deserve to suffer because of their sin? Was God paying them back for years of wrongdoing, for not being holy and righteous, for not being a saved-sanctified-Holy Ghost-filled-fire-baptized-Jesus-on-my-mind type of Christian? Physical suffering was widely viewed as a consequence of sin in the ancient world (cf. Luke 5:18–24; Deut 28–30; Ezek 18:26–27; John 9:2–3) and many today have bought into this thinking. In the Gospel of John, we hear the disciples ask Jesus, "Rabbi, who sinned, this man or his parents, that he was born blind?" (9:2). Suffering, whether from an act of human evil or natural disasters, was correlated with the sin of that individual, community, or family. It was a rational attempt to make sense of why bad things happen to people and how evil can occur when God is supposed to be good. This is the problem of theodicy. This perspective on the marriage of suffering and sin is a way to perhaps affirm that some people deserve their suffering and pain—"it's their fault." It even suggests that some people may be disposable in our eyes, despite their humanity, because we think their lives are a waste.

We so badly want to hold to the idea that good people are prosperous and healthy but evil ones are poor and sick or that loss or lack of success is a sign of divine punishment or that one's financial, social, and physical state are directly linked to one's spiritual state. But this is not true, because God makes the sun rise on the evil and on the good and sends rain on the just and unjust (Matt 5:45). You can't just name a blessing and claim it and get it from God as the proponents of the prosperity gospel want us to believe. God is not a divine genie waiting to grant our every wish. The Galileans who suffered were not worse sinners than all other Galileans. The eighteen killed by the tower of Siloam were not worse offenders than all others in Jerusalem. The tragedy and agony they endured were not due to their sin or a lack of faith or not confessing the Scriptures properly or not thinking positively or not saying their daily morning prayers. Suffering stalks all of us like the paparazzi, and evil sometimes prospers and the righteous suffer. No one is immune from the cancerous sore of suffering, and as New Testament scholar and homiletician Fred Craddock reminds us, "Life in the kingdom is not an elevated game of gaining favors and avoiding losses."[1]

The mention of blood and Pilate in this passage reminds me of how Pilate has on his hands the blood of innocent Jesus, whose crucified suffering comes as a result of following the will and kingdom of God. Jesus did not sin, but he still suffered. The 9/11 World Trade Center towers. The 2004 Indian Ocean tsunami. The 2005 Hurricane Katrina. The 2010 Haiti earthquake. The 2012 Sandy Hook elementary school shooting. Yet, there are those who will say these horrific things happened because "they made a deal with the devil" or "God is paying America back for its sins." That would mean God condones massacres of innocents.

These are silly statements of judgment that present others as worse than us, as if we were saints, and everybody else, sinners. But Jesus turns our wagging finger of judgment toward us and reminds us that there is no hierarchy of sin. We are no better off than others because we, too, must repent. What I condemn in others may just be a reflection of myself. One writer tells a story of how one summer he shared a suite with two other men on a university campus. He writes,

> The suite consisted of two bedrooms, a bath and a living room. The two men occupied one of the bedrooms and I, the other. One night when I came in, as I opened the door, I heard a voice say, "Pipe down, for Pete's sake, pipe down." This was followed by

1. Craddock, *Luke*, 169.

> the soft thud of a pillow being thrown against the wall. In a few minutes one of the fellows stood at the door with disheveled hair and distraught features. "I can't go to sleep. Have you ever heard such snoring? Usually I get off first and then his snoring does not disturb me but tonight he went to bed early. There ought to be a law against it. Why doesn't his wife tell him, or maybe she is a snorer herself." . . . I replied that there was an extra bed in my room, which he could share if my reading lamp would not keep him awake. He accepted gladly, assuring me that the light would not disturb him. After he had retired and I had settled down for an hour's reading, I became aware of his heavy breathing. Then it began—the most pronounced and heavy snoring that I had ever heard in my life. Finally, I could not continue my reading and I knew that sleep would be impossible. I went into the living room, where I spent the night on the couch. . . . When he saw me [in the morning] he said, "Oh no! Don't tell me. I'll never blow my top again about snorers."[2]

In response to the perceived weaknesses of others, we should be humble with this Corinthian awareness: "So if you think you are standing, watch out that you do not fall. No testing has overtaken you that is not common to everyone" (1 Cor 10:12–13). In other words, there are no Olympic champion sinner winners. Sin is sin. It is the spiritual equalizer.

And all suffer because manure happens. Jesus names manure in his parable about the fig tree. He knows that we think manure is disposable, a waste, but he also knows that God runs a waste management program. There is a call to repentance but there is also this parable of divine patience. The vineyard owner tells the gardener that he wants to cut down the fig tree because it hasn't been bearing any fruit. "Why should it be wasting the soil?" What a waste of time. What a waste of energy. What a waste of money. What a waste of space. What a waste of talent. What a waste of a life. Cut it down. It's not worth anything anyway. It's disposable—a waste. We won't miss them if they're massacred or toppled by a crumbling tower. They were a waste, sinners, anyway. But the gracious gardener responds, "Let it alone for one more year, until I dig around it and put manure on it." Give it one more year. One more chance. One more opportunity.

Nothing or no one is a waste when God is involved. There is a wideness and depth to God's mercy, as deep as a mound of manure. Nothing, not even an animal's excrement, is out of the reach and bounds of God's holistic redemptive purposes. We may see others as wasting soil or wasting space on earth because we don't see any fruit, but God chooses to manage

2. Thurman, *Meditations of the Heart*, 40.

waste, to reuse that which others may have discarded. Waste is valuable and not a waste of time to God. Waste can do magic like manure. Manure is an organic fertilizer in agriculture and contributes to the flourishing of the soil by adding nutrients to it. You can't judge a book by its cover. Who would have thought that salvation could come from such a smell? Waste has good purposes when God is gardening. The breadth of God's love provides a wide, gracious space and an opportunity for one to thrive, to bear fruit. "One more year." God does not give up on us. "One more year." Your life may be viewed as a pile of cow mess, but God gets God's hands in messy manure and declares "one more year." God's mercy meets God's judgment in this passage.

It's never too late for redemption. There was "a woman with a spirit that had crippled her for eighteen years. She was bent over and was quite unable to stand up straight." When people saw her, they thought "what a waste." But "when Jesus saw her, he called her over and said, 'Woman, you are set free from your ailment.' When he laid his hands on her, immediately she stood up straight and began praising God" (Luke 13:10ff). "One more year." It's never too late to be straightened out and up, healed and delivered by the hand of Christ. Your life is not a waste nor wasting away because no human life is a waste to God. And God can use whatever is considered to be waste. You are not disposable, no matter what society may say.

One of my oldest cousins has always looked up to me because she could never walk or talk; her gaze always came from below. Her legs are twisted at the kneecaps so if she does move, it is more like a crawl. She, we may say, is differently abled. Many in society may look at her and believe that she is disposable, a waste. But my aunt, her mother, who birthed her into the world, always said, "one more year" even as others may have chanted "cut it down!" She baptized my cousin every time she gave her a warm bath. She served her communion every time she fed her a piece of bread. She clothed her in love every time she dressed her and combed her hair. She affirmed the humanity of my cousin and revealed to her that her life was not a waste, despite the suffering she endured. She was not disposable as my aunt sustained her for "one more year."

Galileans. Jerusalemites. A crippled woman. An older cousin. A child who is differently abled. A senior citizen in hospice. The poor. Orphans. Widows. Prisoners. No one is a waste, out of the reach of God's redemption. This is God's waste management plan—God will save that which others throw away. What we think of as waste may actually be the means of salvation for us—those people, that place, that thing, that waste like manure. Manure has never looked or smelled better than right now.

You can't quit now. When someone sees you, they may see waste. But when God sees you, God sees worth and says, "One more year." You may be struggling through life's weary wilderness, but God says, "One more year." Tears may be your food day and night, but God says, "One more year." All of your hard efforts may never seem to bear fruit, but God says, "One more year." You may feel like you're always climbing up the rough side of the mountain, but God says, "One more year." You may endure a fiery crucible of unexplainable suffering, but God says, "One more year." You may be thinking that life is not worth living anymore, but God says, "One more year." "One more year."

Questions about the Question

- Who might be considered to be a waste in society?
- What is your understanding of sin?
- Why do you think bad things happen to good people?

4

Who will separate us from the love of Christ?

(Rom 8:18–39)

The apostle Paul makes me groan. It's not that I don't like Pastor Paul. Don't get me wrong. It's just that Paul doesn't make it easy to teach from his writings. Paul is, as New Testament scholar Christiaan Beker says, "a man of the proposition, the argument, and the dialogue, not a man of the parable or story."[1] So why in the world am I engaging one of Paul's most theologically argumentative letters?

Paul makes me groan. He's an apocalyptic theologian, though not of the Left Behind series type, who may send people into a twilight zone of a speculative theological orbit never again to hit the ground in any practical, concrete way.

And we've seen how Pastor Paul or at least interpretations of his writings have caused many to groan in despair. There's been a mixed reception of Paul in African American communities historically. Howard Thurman's grandmother refused to listen to any of Paul's letters, except 1 Corinthians 13, because during the time of slavery, the white ministers used Paul to justify slavery.[2] Some have even viewed brother Paul as a patriarchal misogynist. Pastor Paul has made many groan, even perhaps some of you. I

1. Beker, *Paul the Apostle*, 353.

2. Thurman, *Jesus and the Disinherited*, 30–31.

must admit that I used to be one of those Paul naysayers not because I didn't believe Paul but because it seemed as if Paul was more important than Jesus in the academy. And this made no sense to me because without Jesus, Paul would still be Saul.

Nonetheless, I want to confess that I've found a soft place in my hermeneutical heart for the apostle Paul; it helps to have a biblical scholar as a brother! Paul is not more important than Jesus, but Paul can help us understand the gospel of Jesus Christ a bit better. Paul makes me groan because he also shows us that the gospel is in the groan. This won't win him any seminary preaching contests in the age of the health and wealth, painless, prosperity gospel that pimps people for profits. This won't be popular in an era in which we sell worship under the umbrella of the commercialized Christian music industry genre called "praise and worship." There are some who like to get their praise on, but I never hear about anyone getting their "groan on." Worship is not spoiled by tears or tainted by pain.

Paul presents a groaning gospel. Paul won't allow us to avoid "the sufferings of this present time." Paul keeps it real. You don't have to watch *ABC World News Tonight* to find out what's happening in the world. Just read Paul. "The whole creation has been groaning in labor pains until now; and not only the creation, but we ourselves, who have the first fruits of the Spirit, groan inwardly while we wait for adoption, the redemption of our bodies." Humanity is in solidarity with all of creation. Both experience what James Dunn refers to as an "out-of-jointness."[3] Life is out of joint—labor pains and agony and weakness and struggle. The groans of the created order express the presence of pain in the present. Paul does say that the sufferings are "not worth comparing with the glory about to be revealed" but some want to get "glory" without realizing that God's glory is also gory. Groaning is a precursor to glory. One goes through the groans to get to the glory. Good Friday crucifixion before an Easter resurrection. Does your gospel groan? Paul is a truth-telling gospel preacher at this point.

Just look at the pain of the world and listen to creation's groans. Natural disasters. Sociopolitical struggles. Racial and ethnic tensions. Economic divides. Religious conflict. War crimes and their criminals. Heinous acts against children. "The whole creation has been groaning in labor pains and we ourselves groan inwardly." The groaning is not just out there. It is inside of us, too.

We can't escape this interconnected ecology of pain even if we wanted to. We're groaning even as we fill our decorated baskets with trinkets of self-worth to soothe our sorrows, trying to plug the gaping hole in our lives.

3. Dunn, *Theology of Paul the Apostle*, 101.

We try to be "connected" on Facebook and LinkedIn but suffering stalks us. Suffering resides within us even without paying rent. Underneath our privileged pedigree we are perpetually groaning because life is incomplete and unsatisfactory in the valley of heartache. Longing for more. Waiting for more. Groaning for more.

These groans are cosmological and anthropological. But they are also pneumatological. Not even God escapes the groans of pervasive suffering. A groaning God? Hasn't God read Joel Osteen's *Your Best Life Now* or *7 Habits of Highly Effective People* or even Rick Warren's *The Purpose Driven Life*? God needs to get with the painless program! But the Spirit intercedes with sighs too deep for words. "Sighs too deep for words" can be translated "inarticulate groanings." That means God groans too, right alongside all of creation. God does not leave us to our own resources. God does not leave us to drown in tears of despair and carry our burdens alone. God enters into solidarity with us in the midst of our groan-filled agony. Our groans do not isolate us from God but allow us to be more deeply connected with God the Spirit who groans. The Spirit does not avoid suffering. The Spirit is not only on the mountaintops of spiritual ecstasy, but is immersed in the existential agony and messiness of life. God gets down with us in the groan. Not just when I ascend into heaven, God is there. But even when I make my bed in hell, God is there. God groaning for God's own redemption. Paul will not allow us to engage in a form of cheap Christianity that majors in a when-we-all-get-to-heaven-future kind of glory but minors in the nobody-knows-the-trouble-I-see present groans of suffering.

Paul helps us nurture a spirituality of groaning as a mark of what it means to be a Christian and part of God's creation. Yet, these groans don't tell the whole gospel story. They are a prelude to a glorious postlude. A "glory about to be revealed to us," "the revealing of the children of God," "the freedom of the glory of the children of God," "the redemption of our bodies." Pick your phrase. Paul reveals that these groans are going somewhere. They are not stagnant, satisfied with the status quo. They are directional, going to glory, going after glory. Longing, waiting, and hoping, even while groaning, knowing that hope does not disappoint us (Rom 5:5). And the same Spirit who groans also bestows the "first fruits" of eschatological hope, a first installment and pledge of God's future redemption. In the Spirit, the future is present because pneumatology is linked to what has been called by James Forbes the "experience of eschatological epistemology."[4] The Spirit helps us groan and helps us hope. The guts of the groanings are hope because of the Spirit.

4. Forbes, *Holy Spirit and Preaching*, 74–75.

But what in the world is creation groaning for? What is our deepest longing? What is this glory for which we hope? Paul builds his case on one firm foundation in the courtroom of life, and he answers: God's love in Christ Jesus. When he is given the opportunity to expand his argument, he turns to love. "If God is for us, who is against us? He who did not withhold his own Son, but gave him up for all of us, will he not with him also give us everything else?" A God for us and with us. This extravagant love is not cheap but costly. It costs God a Son. This love "for us" hurts. This love for us groans. This love for us dies. A gory glory. Groanings give birth to love in this passage and the same Spirit that groans within us is the same Spirit who sheds God's love in our hearts so we can experience love right now. The Spirit helps us know God's love in Christ. And this love for us is stronger than death and even our groans. So groans give way to a glorious love that words cannot encapsulate.

Love will make you do things you don't normally do. And here, love, God's love, makes Paul a better preacher. It makes Paul a teacher of preaching as he moves in this passage from a homiletical theory of groaning lament to glorious celebration. Paul begins his crescendo at this moment. "Who will separate us from the love of Christ? Will hardship or distress or persecution or famine or nakedness or peril or sword?" He declares a confident "No" because suffering and sorrow will not have the final word in the gospel story, but love will. The love of God. The incomprehensible, incredible, immutable, unconditional, and unstoppable love of God in Christ Jesus. The end of this passage signifies the end of time, when all will be love. In the end is love. Paul is suggesting love wins.

In March 2000, horrendous floods hit the country of Mozambique, leaving many homes and lives threatened and lost. It was a sea of death literally. One woman, Ms. Pedro, climbed into a tree for safety and shelter once the floods overwhelmed her home. Some of her relatives, including her grandmother, were killed in the floods. She was in the tree for three days. Near the end of her time in the tree, on the third day, she gave birth to a daughter.[5] An African tree became a contemporary tree of life. In the midst of the groaning of all creation, in the midst of the sea of death, labor pains gave birth to life and love in the form of a newborn baby. Love wins!

God's love is strong, even stronger than death. "For I am convinced that neither death, nor life, nor angels, nor rulers, nor things present, nor things to come, nor powers, nor height nor depth, nor anything else in all creation, will be able to separate us from the love of God in Christ Jesus our Lord." God's love can't be stopped, won't be stopped. God's love is like the

5. *BBC News*, "Born above the floodwaters."

Energizer Bunny. It keeps going and going and going. God's love in Christ breaks through our barriers and silos of suffering. We groan now but, in the end, we will praise just like Paul because of love.

God's love will lift us to heights we'd never imagine—in the midst of your groaning valley of despair. God's love will meet you, to lift you, to redeem you. Paul experiences God's redeeming love so he praises with a rhetoric of excess, a rhetorical flourish. Unashamed, unrestricted, unmitigated, uncompromising, and I might even add, unseminary-like praise. Love will make you praise in excess with a surplus of meaning. Neither death, nor life, nor angels, nor rulers, nor things present, nor things to come, nor powers, nor height nor depth, nor anything else in all creation. Paul climaxes at this point of his literary offering. Rhetoricians would call this amplification. Homileticians would call this celebration. With my sanctified imagination, I hear music in the subtext of the Pauline text. The Spirit through Paul reaches this height of doxology and celebration because she first engages the depths of human pain and lament. Paul reaches glory because he's already groaned. The cosmological, anthropological, theological groans acknowledge "nobody knows the trouble I see," but the love of God makes Paul declare, "glory, hallelujah." Paul is singing at this moment like a "hallelujah" Christian. It's a German lieder of love, a symphony of love, an ode to love. Do you hear the music that you can't hear with your ears? Maybe it's Bach. Maybe it's Beethoven. Maybe it's the Beatles. Maybe it's Bob Marley. Maybe it's Beyoncé.

No matter the genre, Paul is basically raising the roof as he pumps up the volume of doxology. All because of God's love. This may not make us comfortable, but Paul is not aiming for comfort because God's love has a hold of him. This isn't a time for a sweet and meditative moment of silence in the temple of the Taizé community. Paul has a Pentecostal moment, a Spirit-filled moment, a doxology grounded pneumatologically with an eschatological horizon as he rises to express his love for God because he's loved by God. We're loved by God! He's received something he's been yearning for his whole life, longing for late in the midnight hour, groaning for during his entire ministry—love. He's been groaning for love. We've been groaning for love, the love of God that will not let him or us go. Paul's consumed by divine love and flattened prose won't do for this God who's "so high, you can't get over him, and so low you can't get under him." Paul teaches us about God's love with this heightened sense of theological rhetoric.

And just like a good preacher, just in case we didn't get it the first time, just to make sure we get his point and God's point, Paul basically says the same thing in different ways. He could have just said "nothing will separate us from the love of God in Christ Jesus." Instead, he says, neither death, nor life—any conceivable human condition; nor angels, nor rulers—cosmic or earthly powers; nor things present, nor things to come—not even time can hold back God's love; nor powers; nor height nor depth—as high as you can go and as low as you can go, God is there; nor anything else in all creation will be able to separate us from the love of God in Christ Jesus our Lord. In other words, nothing can separate us from God's love. No matter how deep and wide, wide and deep the groaning fountain in the world or our lives is. Nothing can separate us. No thing. Pick your language—nada, rien, nichts, kitu. It still means the same thing. Nothing. Nothing means nothing. Nothing can stop God from loving you! And remember, this is not the triumph of the groan; this is the triumph of God.

Questions about the Question

- What makes you groan?
- Where do you see suffering in the world?
- Where do you see God's love manifest in the world?

5

Where is the one who is wise?

(1 Cor 1:18–31)

"Consider your own call, brothers and sisters: not many of you were wise by human standards, not many were powerful, not many were of noble birth. But God chose what is foolish in the world to shame the wise; God chose what is weak in the world to shame the strong; God chose what is low and despised in the world, things that are not, to reduce to nothing things that are, so that no one might boast in the presence of God." Who and what God chooses are so interesting. "Not many" in the Corinthian church were powerful civic leaders in Washington, DC, not many were Hollywood celebrities, and not many were the rich and famous of Beverly Hills nor the well-educated of Harvard. There were some known like Crispus, Gaius, and Stephanas, but "not many." Most were unnamed and unfamed and unnoticeable. No PhD, MD, only perhaps a GED. This was the early church. This is the church, supposedly. Consisting of primarily the weak, the lowly, and despised in the world. Paul must be playing a big joke on us, because none of us would apply for a job boasting that we are weak and despised. Rather, we might claim that we are the best of the best. We are the influencers and movers and shakers in the world, the top thought leaders, and the sophisticated Christian intelligentsia, shaping the discourse in our various fields.

But the church is, or at least should be, different. There may be some wise by human standards, some powerful and some of noble birth—but "not many." The vast majority consists of the underwhelming, the underside, and the underappreciated of society. This isn't my ecclesiology, my understanding of the church, this is God's choosing, God's church. God chose what is foolish. God chose what is weak. God chose what is low.

God chooses the despised, the ostracized, and the demonized. It should be of no surprise then that later in this letter to the Corinthian church, we hear Paul admonish them to never say to any part of the body, "I have no need of you," because in Christ's body, everybody is a somebody. There are no nobodies in Christ's body. "On the contrary," Paul says, "the members of the body that seem to be weaker are indispensable, and those members of the body that we think less honorable we clothe with greater honor, and our less respectable members are treated with greater respect, whereas our more respectable members do not need this. But God has arranged the body, giving the greater honor to the inferior member." The inferior and weaker ones—God chooses to honor them and welcome them in the community, for any church will be known by how they treat the most vulnerable in their midst. God chooses and uses the foolish, the weak, the low and despised to reveal his heart. This is a heart, as revealed throughout Scripture, for refugees, strangers, immigrants, widows, orphans, the hungry, the thirsty, the naked, the sick, and the prisoner. God chooses the despised and denigrated to be a part of Christ's body—these are many in Christ's church. Even in Christ's inaugural sermon, his ministry focuses on the poor, the captive, the blind, and the oppressed, the scorned and scorched of the world. God chooses marginal figures as members of Christ's one body.

Those who are despised are destined to make their home with God because God chooses to make room for them in the body. The wisdom of the world may think differently but in the wisdom of God this is the way to unity in the Spirit. The words of the sonnet "The New Colossus," are inscribed on a plaque on the inner wall of the pedestal of the Statue of Liberty. That poem calls the "mighty woman with a torch," the Statue of Liberty, the "Mother of Exiles" and says:

> From her beacon-hand
> Glows world-wide welcome . . .
> Give me your tired, your poor,
> Your huddled masses yearning to breathe free,
> The wretched refuse of your teeming shore.
> Send these, the homeless, tempest-tost to me,
> I lift my lamp beside the golden door![1]

"Not many of you were wise by human standards, not many were powerful, not many were of noble birth. But God chose what is foolish in the world to shame the wise; God chose what is weak in the world to shame the strong;

1. Lazarus, "New Colossus."

God chose what is low and despised in the world," the wretched refuse, and made Christ's church.

Notice that God doesn't build walls but in Christ, has broken down the dividing wall of hostility between people and creates one new humanity, one body in Christ, making peace (Eph 2). The church is a mixed-class community—some named but many unnamed. It doesn't mean there aren't struggles across social strata like we see at the Lord's Supper in the Corinthian church, where one goes hungry and another becomes drunk, revealing tension between the haves and the have-nots. Yet, God chooses to construct a big tent to hold together diversity within the church, in order to work for the unity of the Spirit—rich and poor, male and female, powerful and weak.

Politically, this may all seem foolish, but theologically it is the wisdom of God, a foolish wisdom. "For God's foolishness is wiser than human wisdom, and God's weakness is stronger than human strength." God chooses what is foolish in the world. The Greek word Paul uses for foolishness (*moria*) is the root of the English word "moron." So, one might say that God acts in moronic ways and chooses fools, morons, to do the ministry of Christ in the world. If we take a look at some of the Old Testament prophets, we may learn that God has been working in mysterious ways through fools for centuries. The prophet Isaiah walked naked and barefoot for about three years, predicting a future captivity in Egypt (Isa 20). The prophet Ezekiel lay before a stone, which symbolized struggling Jerusalem, and though God instructed him to eat bread baked on human waste, he asked, ultimately, to use cow dung instead (Ezek 4). And the prophet Hosea married a harlot to symbolize the infidelity of Israel before God (Hos 3). These are not your typical upstanding church members, but they represent the unorthodox, foolish wisdom of God, the morons in God's ministry.

God apparently had gone mad by the looks of it and in early Christianity there was a parody of the method of God's madness and foolishness. The image was called the *alexamenos graffito,* or *graffito blasfemo*. It was carved in the plaster of a wall near the Palatine Hill in Rome. It shows a Christian boy, Alexamenos, being mocked by another boy, or by a group of his school peers. The parody shows a man with a donkey's head being crucified on a tau cross. In front of the cross stands a young man—presumably Alexamenos—raising his hand as if in prayer. At the top of the picture, are the words, "Alexamenos worships his God." His God is in the form of a man with a donkey's head hanging on a cross. In antiquity, though it was applauded for being hardworking, the donkey was also mocked for being stupid. Eventually, the donkey became the regular metaphor for stupidity and foolishness. In Christianity, there was a tradition claiming that Joseph and Mary fled with the child to Egypt on a donkey, although this specific detail is never indicated in the Bible. The donkey was venerated for many generations as a vehicle for salvation. Even in his triumphal entry into Jerusalem, Jesus rode on the back of a donkey, fulfilling the prophecy of Zechariah, carrying overtones of foolishness, and representing Christ's carnivalesque parody of worldly power and authority. The donkey has always been a part of the foolish history of God—thus the message of a crucified Christ and its foolishness is captured in this carved image of a crucified donkey-God. It was laughable, foolish, and absurd. This was the folly of the cross caught in an unforgettable image, merging the crucified Christ with a donkey.

"Not many of you were wise by human standards, not many were powerful, not many were of noble birth. But God chose what is foolish in the world to shame the wise . . ." God chooses dumb donkeys. Just as God used Balaam's ass, God still uses the same creatures today in the form of human beings. But as that ancient plaster depiction shows, donkeys, the fools of God, the moron ministers, end up hanging out to dry and die on a cross. Fools get ridiculed but they also get crucified.

Yet God chooses donkeys, chooses the weak, chooses the low and despised, chooses the word of the cross to be the power of God. A cross was a symbol of failure and public embarrassment as it was a tool, an ancient form of death row, used to enforce the *Pax Romana*, Roman imperial peace. Revolutionaries, terrorists, criminals, slaves were punished on it and made laughingstocks of society. To be put on a cross meant ugliness, contempt, weakness, loser, unpatriotic scumbag. It was where donkeys belonged. But God chooses the cross and lands on it, becoming a crucified Christ, the means of salvation and the revelation of the power of God. A crucified Christ was an oxymoron. God is a moron, is foolish, has gone mad, is so mad, madly in love with the world for which Christ died. It makes no worldly sense but that's the method of God's madness—a grotesque death to bring us the glory of God and life everlasting—and through the foolishness of the proclamation of Christ crucified, save the world.

A crucified donkey God is the means of salvation. God does things on God's own terms so we would boast in God and find our source of life in Jesus Christ. All of our credentials are crucified with the donkey and we find ourselves by losing ourselves in the foolish wisdom of God and the foolishness of the cross. We discover life at and on the cross with the foolish, with the weak, with the low and despised, the donkeys of today's world, the outcasts, the victims, the huddled masses, the wretched refuse, the migrants who have nowhere to lay their heads, the Christ. The cross of Christ reminds us and tells the truth, not alternative facts, that not many of us are wise by human standards, not many of us are powerful, not many of us are of noble birth, but many of us are morons in the ministry of Jesus. We are fools in Christ's body, donkeys on a mission.

As such, Christians don't believe in ourselves or country, we believe in God and worship God, a God whose work confounds the wisdom of the world. As worshippers of this God who displays radical foolish love on a cross, we, too, are followers of this chief fool in heaven. When we pray in the Lord's Prayer, "on earth as it is in heaven," this is a call to bring this divine foolishness to earth and to be mad with the love of God, so mad that you become a fool of the faith, a moron for Jesus in the Spirit. Just as God was so foolish as to choose us, we're called to choose the weak and choose the low and despised. To choose to do justice, and to love kindness, and to walk humbly with our God. To choose to speak the truth from our hearts. To choose to be a fool for unconditional love and mercy. To choose hope.

Be that donkey that carries the light of the crucified risen Christ into the streets. Bring the madness because God is mad, a fool, a mighty moron, making the world right. "Lord, I want to be a Christian in my heart." In other words, "Lord, I want to be a moron for you." Where are the donkeys? I know there was one on a cross. I hope you are one, too.

Questions about the Question

- How would you describe the wisdom of the world?
- Why is it difficult to choose the foolish way of God?
- How can we be morons for God's foolishness?

6

Who is worthy to open the scroll and break its seals?

(Rev 5:1–14)

The hymn "Lift Every Voice and Sing" speaks a human truth for many in one of its lyrics: "We have come over a way that with tears has been watered." Tears have moistened the soil of many people's journeys. Some have lived the words of Saint Augustine, who in his *Confessions* tells of how his tears flowed so freely that they made a pillow for his heart.[1] For others, it may be more like the psalmist who ate his tears for breakfast, lunch, and dinner—my "tears are my food day and night."

John is drinking his tears as they flood his life. He's drenched. He's baptized in tears of desperation. The pages of this passage are damp with the water of sorrow. If we look at John's canonical face close enough, we will see the tracks of his tears. I learned that notion from the great musical Motown theologian, Smokey Robinson. "So take a good look at my face, you'll see my smile looks out of place, if you look closer, it's easy to trace the tracks of my tears." Smokey spoke about the meaning behind this song. He said that if you looked at someone's face close enough, you could see the tracks left behind by their tears because they had cried so much.

John has cried so much that you can see his tracks even from far away through the binoculars of biblical history. That's not sweat on his face. Those

1. Augustine, *Confessions*, IX.12, 202.

are tears. I can almost hear his crying turning into moaning. At first glance, we might think John is in his first year of seminary because he's weeping bitterly; but he's weeping because he meets his own finitude and powerlessness. His tears are a fatalistic flood of lost hope, not because of a seminary experience, but because he can't see the future. It's unknown. John weeps bitterly because he doesn't have power over his own future. He can barely go on with life as it is because his future is out of his hands. Every teardrop represents human weakness, so there he is drowning in this pool of agony and uncertain reality.

John understands human limitations and frailty because "no one in heaven or on earth or under the earth was able to open the scroll or to look into it." The scroll was the book of destiny about God's will. The scroll was God's final plan for the world. The scroll represents God's future for us and no one could open these pages about the future of human history. No one could sneak a peek into God's plan. No one, nowhere. Not Oprah Winfrey or Barack Obama or Bill Gates or Martha Stewart or Donald Trump or Simon Cowell or Paula Abdul or Beyoncé or P. Diddy or your daddy or mommy, husband or wife, son or daughter. No one, nowhere. Not Calvin, Luther, Barth, King, or Cone will help either. Not even Wall Street. The US government can't bail John out because they can't even see into the future! No one knows what is to come. John is trapped in wet chains of fear and hopelessness.

And we should be weeping right along with John, not because of fear of the unknown, but because we have fooled ourselves into thinking we can save ourselves and the world. All of that talk about God has made some of us think we are god. When the mighty angel asks, "Who is worthy to open the scroll and break its seals?" we raise our hands to be first in line. We clothe ourselves in the garments of academic credentials or in the garb of "how many things I'm doing for Jesus" or in the religious clothes of self-assurance or in the cloak of a theological or political camp. I'm this or I'm that. I'm leading this, doing that, teaching this and helping with that. That we soon forget who really has the power, who really is in control, who really is in charge, who really is Lord. "No one in heaven or on earth or under the earth was able to open the scroll or to look into it." But we still build our human thrones, thinking we have the power. Building our thrones, those symbols of the center of the cosmos, making ourselves the center of an ecclesial universe. Our thrones grow second by second, minute by minute as if to change the words of that hymn and sing "Immortal, invisible, I'm only wise." Not what I can do for the church but what the church can do for me. "Crown me with many crowns." No wonder John is weeping as he sets his tearful gaze on us out of the pages of Scripture and still says there is "no one."

John's weeping, because if we continue on this prideful path, we will dig our own graves to nowhere but down. John has good reason to weep if all there is, is human finite power. He has good reason to weep if we are in control. He has good reason to weep if all there is, is us. We might as well throw in the theological towel if we are in charge, if we have ultimate power, if we hold the future, if that's what we're teaching in our classrooms and churches. John has good reasons to weep at our self-deception, thinking that we have the power to make a better future. We don't even have the power to make a better present. John weeps until his eyes, blinded by despair, are made to see who really has the power over our future, and what he sees may surprise us. It's not Mary's pretty little lamb whose fleece was white as snow, but a Lamb whose fleece is red with blood for you and me. His shed tears cannot compare with the shed blood of a Lamb. John realizes then, in the words of James Weldon Johnson, that "we have come treading a path through the blood of the slaughtered."[2]

A Lamb standing as if it had been slaughtered. A lame Lamb? Where are the prosperity gospel gurus now? A lame Lamb? Where are those who want to bleach Christ squeaky clean? A lame Lamb? Where are those who want to praise without acknowledging pain? A lame Lamb. Mary's crucified Lamb of God, Jesus Christ. Broken, bruised, beat down for us. "Nothing in his appearance that we should desire him . . . like a sheep that before its shearers is silent" (Isa 53). Slaughtered but still standing. This weak-looking lamb has the power, all power in his nail-pierced hands. He is worthy, able and authorized, to open the scroll of the future and its seven seals. He holds the future in his hands. God's future for us. There is a future, and this future is not closed. There is a hope John never fully realized until he saw the One who has the scroll in his hands. The slaughtered, standing Lamb has the power. The power to help our economic situation, the power to help our healthcare system, the power to help our educational system, the power to help our governmental system, the power to help even our church system, the power to give us a future, the power to make all things new and the power to make all things right. I've got the power? He's got the power! Wonder-working power in the blood of the Lamb!

Once the Lamb shows up, the pages of this pericope dry up John's tears but are now stained with blood. Our future is costly so there is no room for cheap praise, for as Gordon Lathrop reminds us "The grounds of our thanksgiving are found in a crucified man."[3] The presence of the crucified Lamb changes John's existential melodic key from minor to major. There's

2. Johnson, "Lift Every Voice and Sing."

3. Lathrop, *Holy Things*, 58.

a new song beginning to bubble within his soul. Do you hear what I hear? When the Lamb "went and took the scroll from the right hand of the one who was seated on the throne" then the praise party begins, the musical melodies of the harp begin to be plucked, the aromatic prayers of the saints start going up, and then my favorite part begins—singing, full-voiced singing of a real hallelujah chorus. There is really no other appropriate response to the realization that the Lamb holds our future securely in his hands. The Lamb is the fulcrum of our future. John's tears didn't drop in vain for every teardrop was an epiclesis for God to intervene. John discovers they that sow in tears will reap with joy. Weeping may endure for the night, but joy comes in the morning. And with joy, comes much singing. John is singing now in the celestial chorus of the crucified One. Do you hear what I hear?

There is our wounded song leader, our saving maestro himself, with his slaughtered stance, in the center of this chorus, leading us in a victory chant. Holding the scroll, leading us in this scrollful song. I see that scroll becoming a bloodstained baton, directing us in our primary doxological vocation. And with every wave of his baton, the singing gets louder, and the choir grows in number. With each wave, he wipes every tear from every eye. Death will be no more, mourning and crying and pain will be no more. His only instruction is "do not weep." No more weeping John. Just lots of full-voiced singing because we know who holds the future. Do you hear what I hear? A beautiful heavenly choir of living creatures and elders who sing in harmonious hymnic counterpoint, "You are worthy to take the scroll and to open its seals, for you were slaughtered and by your blood you ransomed for God saints . . . you have made them to be a kingdom and priests serving our God." This was spontaneous, this new song they never rehearsed but they sang it in tune. They never sang it before, but it sure felt right. It was a song of freedom; their Deliverer had come. Like in South Africa, "Freedom is coming. Freedom is coming. Freedom is coming, oh yes I know."

Through a kingly sacrificial Lamb, freedom comes. This is the song of the redeemed, not for a segregated spiritual click, but for the "saints from every tribe and language and people and nation." We might be surprised who's singing with us. No economy of exclusion there, no demonization of difference there, those we thought shouldn't be there, those we didn't want to be there, they are there, God's diverse kingdom. The loosed chains of oppression and sin are stirring up every crack and crevice of society and every corner of heaven. We've been set free to sing! Do you hear what I hear? "I heard the voice of many angels surrounding the throne and the living creatures and the elders; they numbered myriads of myriads and thousands of thousands, singing with full voice, 'Worthy is the Lamb that was slaughtered to receive power and wealth and wisdom and might and honor and glory and blessing!'" This cosmic choir keeps growing into the thousands and keeps growing in volume. The loud, full-voiced singing can't stop, won't stop because deliverance has come Christ-style. There's a whole new world. A whole new way of living. A future and a hope. A slain Lamb conquers. The last are now first. The least, the greatest. The slaves become kings. The poor become priests. This is the reason why we sing—the Lamb holds our future.

This might be bad news for some because this song of redemption is also a song of resistance. It's not just a rap for God but it is as Brian Blount puts it, a "rap against Rome,"[4] the Roman emperors then and now, the imperialistic gods that oppress and depress. This ministry of song says up to God but down to other gods—the gods of a financial fiscal year that would say "you don't have enough money to do your ministry anymore." The gods that would say "your vocation is really a career, so you should just strive to be a big steeple preacher with little theology." The gods of profit rather than being a prophet of God. This song calls you to give voice against all the powers that would try to mute your voice—this is praise against the powers. I know it's not popular, or cute, but Christ is the musical conductor. This is a song you should have in your musical ministerial repertoire because it declares the demise of the gods. The gods will not prevail because there is just one slaughtered, standing Lamb, and the future is his. Sing the future now. Sing the future present.

This sanctified song won't make it to the top of the *Billboard* charts but it's still contagious. You might not hear it right now but it's beginning to rumble. This song can't be stopped because there is a Power operating in the world that is greater than any human power. This song won't be stopped because of the Lamb of God who takes away the sins of the world. He's got the scroll! Do you hear what I hear? I hear the heavens vibrating as others join in the holy refrain. The angels, the elders, the living creatures are fired up. In the prelude, there were lots of tears, but if you looked at the tear-tracking system now, you would see that in the postlude, the stormy clouds of tears have given way to sunny doxological cheers. And if you listen closely, I hear something beginning to rumble.

I hear John singing but he's not alone. I hear Oprah Winfrey, Barack Obama, Bill Gates, Martha Stewart, Donald Trump, Simon Cowell, Paula Abdul, Beyoncé, P. Diddy, fathers, mothers, husbands, wives, sons, daughters, Calvin, Luther, Barth, King, Cone, Wall Street, and even the US government. No one is left out of this hymn sing. I hear the birds in the air chirping. The cows in the field mooing. The dogs in the neighborhood barking. The cats down the street meowing. "Every creature in heaven and

4. Blount, *Can I Get A Witness?*, 91.

on earth and under the earth and in the sea, all that is in them," singing not "me, myself, and I" but "To the one seated on the throne and to the Lamb be blessing and honor and glory and might forever and ever!" Amen! Amen! The future is God's and don't you forget it!

Questions about the Question

- What societal influences make us believe we have ultimate power?
- What stories have created the tracks of your tears?
- What is your rap song for God?

2

WHO AM I?

7

Why do I live?

(Genesis 25:19–34)

I could talk about Jacob and Esau, who usually steal the biblical spotlight in this narrative. They're twins in tension. One will be stronger than the other, and the elder shall serve the younger. As the youngest in my family, I really like that last part. I hope my oldest brother is paying attention! Esau loved hunting outdoors. Jacob was a quiet man who loved the indoors of his tent. Esau was first and hairy and red and loved to eat red stuff. Jacob is second and grabbed Esau's heel. He's a fierce, shrewd little rascal who holds his foodie brother hostage to food for his birthright. To make things worse, Mom and Dad get involved in this brotherly battle. Isaac loved Esau but Rebekah loved Jacob.

I could talk more about Isaac, whose age gets attention as if he's the one who has to give birth; it's obvious the writer of Genesis is not a woman. Isaac was sixty years old when the twins were born. But I'm pretty sure that having twins is not number one on your bucket list of things to do near retirement. I could say a lot more about Isaac or the twins.

But Rebekah raises the piercing question for our reflection. "If it is to be this way, why do I live?" Why do I live? Not "how" should I live, but why? Like Sarah before her and Rachel after her, Rebekah was barren. Her husband was a child of promise (21:1–7) and she was from good family stock (25:20), but even that was not an antibiotic against emptiness and disappointment. Privileged pedigree can't prevent pain. In a patriarchal society, barrenness was not a positive thing as it was thought that having children added value to womanhood. But then the Lord answers Isaac's prayer and intervenes to allow Rebekah to conceive. This should be great news after twenty years of waiting to have a baby and now she's even having twins. But we learn that "the children struggled together within her." That experience is what causes her to ask the ancient question that has contemporary relevance— "if it is to be this way, why do I live?" Rebekah is caught in a web of suffering.

First, the pain of barrenness. Then, the pain of struggle between her sons. It's as if her suffering is eternal and inescapable. She was "tossed about, with many a conflict, many a doubt, fightings and fears within, without."[1] There was a struggle within her but then to see her twin sons battle over the family legacy must have killed her. Two very different children from the same mother and father. One a CEO of a Fortune 500 company; the other locked up in prison for selling drugs in a red light district. "If it is to be this way, why do I live?" My barrenness was broken in order to create brokenness in my family? If I can never experience the bounty of joy, why live? Is there any reason for living if my struggle and pain never go away and every time I turn around there's another problem? If I can't escape the pain, what's the point? Why do I live? Like a person contemplating suicide as a means to stop the pain, Rebekah asks a question that may be on our mind—why do I live?

When our pain seems to be from everlasting to everlasting in a perpetual cycle of suffering, we may ask this question too. Conflict permeates this narrative as it does our lives. Job was right when he said, "Human beings are born to trouble just as birds fly upward" (Job 5:7). Just because there is a promise from the God of Abraham does not mean there won't be pain—Rebekah reveals this. Just because we may be chosen by God does not mean we will live a trouble-free life. The call of God may include a call to strife and struggle and confrontation. Being a Christian is not the eschewal of pain. We can't romanticize the Christian faith to think that it only includes blessings; there are burdens to bear as well. To be a Christian means to be a cross-bearer, and if you make the sign of the cross, you are marking yourself with a symbol of suffering. There is no way around it when one serves a God whose salvific means includes a bloody cross. Howard Thurman wrote that "pain has a ministry"[2] in that the fact of pain may help us understand life in a fuller way.

Life is not well-manicured and pedicured. It is not perfect sans struggle. We are confronted with the presence of suffering in the Christian life

1. Elliott, "Just As I Am."
2. Thurman, *Meditations of the Heart*, 65.

and suffering is only a scandal if one assumes Christianity bears no scars on its historical body and Christ bears no scars on his resurrected body. Now this does not mean that God sends suffering or causes it. One theologian tells us that "God's gracious will for his creatures—his willing of all things to his own infinite goodness—is the creative power that makes all things to be and the consummate happiness to which all things are called; but this does not (indeed, must not) mean that everything that happens is merely a direct expression of God's desire for his creatures or an essential stage within the divine plan for history."[3] He goes further to say that there is no need to provide "a divine rationale for every dimension of every event in which [God's] creatures are involved, no matter how much those events might reflect that ultimate privation, evil."[4] This understanding is in direct opposition to the notion that God's goodness is realized not just in spite of but by way of cruelty, misery, and catastrophe. God does not ordain pain and commission it into the world.

Yet, the struggle is still real within Rebekah and inside and outside of us. It's there and cannot be denied. Suffering makes an indelible stamp on the world and on Christian discipleship. But we should not pray to suffer as a masochistic means to union with Christ, because just as Christ prayed, we naturally plead, "Take this cup from me" (Luke 22:42). Suffering is a fact, and it is not necessarily redemptive. Think of the most horrific story of death or pain you have ever heard; many times, it's not redeemable.

"If it is to be this way . . ." This way, this path I must travel. My child has cancer. My parent has dementia. I struggle with mental illness. "I do not do what I want, but I do the very thing I hate . . . for I do not do the good I want, but the evil I do not want is what I do" (Romans 7:19). "If it is to be this way, why do I live?"

Rebekah, like us, can't make sense of her suffering and maybe believes somehow that human life should not include pain and suffering. Belief in a painless existence could be a product of bowing down to a sanitized, Clorox-bleached Christ. We're not saved to escape suffering in this life nor are we called by God for ourselves. That may be part of the problem in this selfie generation. We have forgotten why we truly live or for whom we live. In the selfie technological orbit, it might appear that we live to see ourselves because it is all about the self. See my new haircut. See my new outfit. See my bircher muesli breakfast. See my dog sleeping. See my dog jumping. See my dog wagging his tail. See me with my dog. I just woke up. I just returned from a jog in record time. I just repainted and redesigned my office. See my

3. Hart, *Doors of the Sea*, 97–98.

4. Hart, *Doors of the Sea*, 98.

office. It is a "see me" era and the technological gadgets have rightly been called "iGods."[5]

iBook, iMac, iPod, iPhone, iPad. i. When Steve Jobs first introduced the iMac in 1998, he said that the "i" stood for internet, individual, instruct, inform, inspire. If one bows to these iGods it may feed into the overemphasis on "i" and it is a little, lowercased "i." Little because perhaps we have been reduced to a smaller size following these gods, particularly the individual "i" that is consumed by selfies when we shouldn't really be gazing only at ourselves but at the face of God. It is when we encounter God, like Isaiah in the temple (Isa 6), that we may begin to see ourselves for who we really are and recognize why we live. If we only do selfies, it fosters an i-world where our lives revolve around ourselves, when in fact the self is not actually the real goal.

The apostle Paul reminds us in Galatians that "it is no longer I who live, but Christ who lives in me" (Gal 2:20). I but not I. Our identity becomes more whole with God's presence and with Christ in us, our lives take on his mission, even if we suffer, even "If it is to be this way . . ."

I want to suggest that there was something within Rebekah that was bigger than Rebekah, despite everything she endured. The question, "Why do I live?" may seem to be only about the individual self and in a selfie generation it may be difficult to imagine beyond our i-universe, but even God tells Rebekah, "Two nations are in your womb." Edom and Israel. She may not have even understood what was happening, but nations were a product of Rebekah's life. Her life was more than her life. There was a larger purpose within her that went beyond her because even in the midst of struggle God was at work in and through her in the larger story of salvation of the world.

This is a reminder that we are not our own (1 Cor 6), but we belong to God. As the song says, "My life is not my own, to you I belong, I give myself, give myself to you." "Here I am, Lord." I do not own my life; I am a steward of the life that I have been given. We are servants of Christ. We are a part of God's story of salvation thus our lives are not for us; they are for God. Why do I live? We live for God. Some may say, "I live to eat, drink, and be merry. I live to work. I live for my family. I live to be loved. I live to serve and do good. I live to discover the latest innovation in technology. I live to find a cure for cancer." Some of these are noble goals, but our Christian vocation, the reason we live, has to do with God and what God desires for the redemption of the world. We can't say like William Ernest Henley, "I am the master of my fate, I am the captain of my soul," because we live for God.

5. See Detweiler, *iGods*.

What or who you live for says something about what or who you will die for. Why do I live? Why do you live? There may be much struggle in your life these days and we can't rationalize or explain away the suffering. Yet there is a purpose within you bigger than you—as big as the world God came to redeem in Christ. God loved the world that he gave his only Son. To save the world includes conflict, tension, suffering, and death. God has reasons that human reason will never know.

And God is not into selfies. God is into us, into us so much that God became one of us and took on our pain. "He was despised and rejected by others; a man of suffering . . . acquainted with infirmity . . . wounded for our transgressions, crushed for our iniquities, upon him was the punishment that made us whole, and by his bruises we are healed" (Isa 53:5). So much suffering that Jesus even asked his own "why" question: "My God, my God, why have you forsaken me?" (Matt 27:46).Why do I live to die? We are not alone. Jesus asks Rachel's and our question, and we live to answer his question for we are the answer. He died for us that we might live.

We live for God despite what we may endure but God lived, died, rose, and lives for us, forever. Who God died for says something about who God lives for, eternally. It is to be this way and because of it, I do live and "I know that my redeemer lives and that in the end he will stand on the earth" (Job 19:25). Why do I live? "Because he lives, I can face tomorrow; because he lives, all fear is gone; because I know who holds the future and life is worth the living just because he lives."[6]

Questions about the Question

- What are you living for?
- What is the larger purpose of your life that is being born within you?
- What are the internal or external struggles you are dealing with these days?

6. Gaither and Gaither, "Because He Lives."

8

Why do we fast, but you do not see?

(Isa 58:1–12)

There is a genre of fast food that is God's fast food. This isn't about consuming communion elements or a Methodist hymnal or the Book of Common Prayer. This isn't a medical study of our physical eating habits and the number of pounds we gain or lose by eating this fast food. We won't be examining our stomachs but our hearts. God's fast food leads us to interrogate our worship diet. Many of us have probably been on a diet, are on a diet, or someone we know thinks we ought to be on a diet. We think diets make us feel good, but most of all, look good. There are so many diets available these days, making all kinds of promises. But the worship diet is not about looks; it's about love—the love of God and love of neighbor. In many religious traditions, including Christianity, there is the spiritual practice of fasting, a fast diet, a worship diet, where one abstains from food in order to improve one's own spiritual life before God.

Israel engages in this type of fast. They abstain from food and wear the sackcloth and ashes as a sign of mourning and penance. They are liturgically literate and ritually right. They want to draw closer to God and this is the way they know how to do it from their catechism classes in Sunday school. This is how they've done worship for years—sing the right song, say the right prayer, do the right dance, say "Amen" at the right time. But they seem to move further away from God as they dive deeper into themselves, deeper into their own worship pattern. They can't figure out why their fasting won't work. "Why do we fast, but you do not see? Why humble ourselves, but you do not notice?" Someone today might say, "I have a full worship diet of Christianity in my life. I go to church. I sing beautiful hymns, and say lovely prayers of confession, and serve the communion elements from time to time, and pay my tithes, and attend worship committee meetings where we talk about the last committee meeting where we talked about the last committee meeting. I help with fellowship meals whenever we have them. I pray before my meals at home and even before I go to bed. I read my Bible every day, early in the morning of course, and sometimes I even fast like Israel, but God, where are you?"

Israel can't figure out what's wrong with their worship diet until God speaks—"You serve your own interest on your fast day and oppress all your workers. You fast only to quarrel and to fight and to strike with your fists. Is this the fast I choose, a day to humble oneself? Will you call this a fast, a day acceptable to the Lord?" God brings a serious liturgical critique against Israel. Israel's fast diet is an abstention, not just from food, but from others. They delight in God but despise God's people. They abstain from loving their neighbor and feed on a worship diet of selfish, individualistic living that regards no one else but themselves. Somehow their ritual ethic becomes disconnected from a righteous ethic. Their fasting leads them quickly toward ethical negligence because religious ritual without a social outlook can become only self-serving. Israel reveals how tempting it is to believe that performing holy acts like fasting or proximity to holy things like a church or a Bible or the sacraments, make us holy. It's idolatry when we make our liturgical or spiritual practices or objects little idols, because it's really a turn to ourselves bowing at our own altar, rather than turning to God, which is also a turn outward toward others in need.

What Israel has done is create God in their own image and remix the traditional hymn and sing, "Crown Me with Many Crowns." They neglect serving others, mistreat and bully them with violent acts. Their spiritual liturgical diet is navel-gazing at their stomachs full of self at the throne of narcissism. They serve their own interests, while disregarding others. They're satisfied with a status quo Christian spirituality that has no impact on society when the gospel is personal, communal, and social. They are only concerned with the liturgy and not the liturgy after the liturgy. And so they beat and tear down anyone and anything on their way up towards the pearly gates of heaven. They sing, "I'll fly away, Oh glory, I'll fly away, when I die hallelujah by and by" as they wave bye-bye to their neighbor in need.

But is this just Israel's story or is it ours, too? Has Israel's liturgical approach been our practical theology of worship all along? I mean one in which we think that just coming to a Sunday service or a Wednesday night prayer meeting or attending a Bible study or a Christian education class is the totality of what it means to worship God, and if we don't like the preaching, the singing, the praying, the liturgy, the choir robes, the way communion is administered, we can go somewhere else, window shopping for a church that we like because it suits our interests, shopping at what Yale professor Bryan Spinks calls the "worship mall"?[1] In this consumeristic age, we may struggle with selfishness and desire only "self-maximization."[2] Might it be that our worship diet neglects others often and we possess an anorexic theology of worship, thin on God's love for the world? It may look like worship and sound like worship and feel like worship but if concrete love of neighbor is not included as part of our regular diet of worship, it isn't worship! Why do we fast, worship, and you do not see? Maybe our worship only reflects and reinforces our own interests and not God's interest in giving oneself for the sake of the world.

"Immortal, invisible, I'm only wise?" If that is the case, we're on the wrong kind of worship diet, a destructive diet that distances ourselves from others when in fact our Sunday worship of God is only authenticated by how we live for God Monday through Saturday in the world. If we gaze out at our world today, instead of Dr. King's dream of a beloved community, holding hands and singing, we seem to be living a nightmare with a disturbing breach, not "coming together," not realizing our lives are interdependent, but seeing, in the words of the Nigerian novel, "things fall apart."[3] They are falling apart because we may be serving our own interests even when it comes to worship. We get liturgical fast food only for ourselves in the drive thru of oppressive selfishness. And as we look at the menu, we experience theological amnesia, and forget that someone else is hungry, homeless, and naked, walking the path of destructive selfishness. "Why do we fast, but you do not see?"

God sees clearly actually, but God's worship diet includes a different kind of fast food. "Is not this the fast that I choose: to loose the bonds of injustice, to undo the thongs of the yoke, to let the oppressed go free, and to break every yoke? Is it not to share your bread with the hungry, and bring the homeless poor into your house; when you see the naked, to cover them, and not to hide yourself from your own kin?" (Isa 58:6–7). God redefines what fasting is by moving beyond the practice itself to including the freedom of and provision for other people. God calls for worship, fasting, as selfless giving. God calls for worship as service in the world. God tells Israel, "Your fasting is about abstention, even abstaining from doing justice, but my

1. Spinks, *Worship Mall.*

2. Scharen, *Faith as a Way of Life*, 13.

3. Achebe, *Things Fall Apart.*

worship is about participation, engagement, doing justice for others, walking in love towards another. My worship is having your life service match your lip service. My worship includes social witness and social justice. My worship diet incorporates your entire life. My worship diet plan will help the world that I love." God reframes fasting, therefore worship, as a way of life, not a particular day or a singular practice. God-centered worship will lead to "opposition to injustice, liberation from oppressive systems, the sharing of resources, and the growth of community."[4] Loving God means loving one's neighbors (Matt 22:37–40).

With this understanding, fasting, worship, is service, so when you leave a worship service, there's another worship service, another liturgy after the liturgy, where we engage in worship by doing the mission of God in the world. If our service inside becomes severed from our service outside, then we lose liturgical integrity because our creeds don't match our deeds and we make hypocrisy holy. It is not worship *and* ethics, but God's fast food challenges us to see worship *as* ethics. Fasting is action. Worship is a verb. If there is any abstention in this form of fasting, it is the abstaining from indifference and inactivity and egotism because right worship is righteous living committed to others, especially the least of these. This worship diet is for the common good. Dr. King was on this diet and said one of the most urgent questions is, "What did you do for others?"[5] That is the question of the hour as we check ourselves before we wreck ourselves liturgically. What are you doing for others?

And God didn't say that they had to be Christian in order to be helped. God didn't say that they had to have the same skin color or same language to be helped. God didn't say that to be helped they had to believe the same thing you believe or like the same things you like. Need is no respecter of persons! God just said that the food for the fast diet is to loose the bonds of injustice, undo the thongs of the yoke, let the oppressed go free, give bread to the hungry, a home to the homeless, clothes to the naked, and love to somebody.

And the good news is that God is right there, inhabiting our worship as we serve. After God redefines fasting and gives the challenge, the prophet declares, "Then your light shall break forth like the dawn, and your healing shall spring up quickly . . . Then you shall call, and the Lord will answer; you shall cry for help, and he will say, Here I am" (Isa 58:8–9). God actually is found among the oppressed. "Here I am. Right with the least of these. Right with the hungry, the homeless, the naked, the outcast. Right with that

4. van Harn, *Lectionary Commentary*, 372.

5. King, "Three Dimensions of a Complete Life."

person you don't want to touch and rather ignore. Right on the margins. That's where you'll find me if you eat my fast food. Here I am, conducting the liturgy of liberation. Here I am. I'm Immanuel. Here I am. You won't be alone in your service. Here I am, putting in the proper ingredients in your worship diet of love and justice. Here I am, still making my fast food for the poor and widows. Here I am with the least, the last, the left out. Here I am in the trenches of trouble, but this shouldn't surprise you."

"Here I am." "I was hungry and you gave me food, I was thirsty and you gave me something to drink, I was a stranger and you welcomed me, I was naked and you gave me clothing, I was sick and you took care of me, I was in prison and you visited me . . . just as you did it to one of the least of these who are members of my family, you did it to me" (Matt 25). "This is where you will find me. Here I am—you thought you were serving me, but I am serving you. I am meeting your need. I am rebuilding your ruined society through your service. Your light shall break forth like the dawn. Your healing shall spring up quickly. Your light shall rise in the darkness. Your gloom will be like the noonday. Your bones will be made strong. You shall be like a watered garden. Your ancient ruins shall be rebuilt; you shall be called the repairer of the breach, the restorer of streets to live in. That can't happen without me. That can't happen without my fast. You'll call and cry for help and I'll answer. Here I am."

Among just, reordered relationships, recognizing that our healing is linked with the healing of others, God is present and glory shines. That light shines as the breach of brokenness in a society is bridged and healed. Where there is reconciliation, God is and God's light shines. This is God's promise to us. That when we work to repair the breach between us and our neighbors by repairing the divide between our worship practices and mission in the world, God is present, restoring what was damaged and ravaged to create an eternal communal harmony. Our society and its streets will be full of peace and the light of this world will be no other than the glory of the Lord (Isa 60:1–2). "*If* you remove the yoke from among you, the pointing of the finger, the speaking of evil, *if* you offer your food to the hungry and satisfy the needs of the afflicted, *then* your light shall rise" because your life will be the "amen" to the proclamation on your lips and you can then stand and sing on Sundays the praises of our hidden Lord and worship with integrity.

Natalia Dmitruk exemplified great integrity in 2004 in the Ukraine when Victor Yushchenko stood for the presidency there. He was opposed by the ruling party, had his face disfigured and was mysteriously poisoned. Yet this could not deter him from running for the presidency. On the day of the election, Yushchenko had a comfortable lead, but the ruling party would not have any of that and tampered with the results. The state-run television station reported, "Ladies and gentlemen, we announce that the challenger Victor Yushchenko has been decisively defeated." In the lower right-hand corner of that same TV shot, Natalia Dmitruk was translating for the deaf community and as the news presenter reported the lies of the regime, Dmitruk refused to translate them. Rather, she signed, "I'm addressing all the deaf citizens of Ukraine . . . They are lying and I'm ashamed to translate those lies. Yushchenko is our president." This led the deaf community to spread this message via text about the fabrications and as the news spread about Dmitruk's act of courage and truth, other journalists were inspired to do the same and tell the truth. Eventually, the "Orange Revolution" occurred, in which a million people wore orange and went to the capital city of Kiev to call for a new election. When a new election was held, Victor Yushchenko became president.[6]

One small act of integrity in the corner of a big TV screen can make a world of difference and make the world different. Be the word you proclaim. Be the difference you've been waiting for.

Questions about the Question

- Why is fasting difficult?
- Where are the social breaches in the world?
- How does God's definition of fasting fit with your understanding?

6. Boggs, "FIRST-PERSON." The historical context of this moment is also recounted at http://content.time.com/time/subscriber/article/0,33009,1009663,00.html.

9

Is there no balm in Gilead?

(Jer 8:18–9:1)

I once heard it said that "Jeremiah was a bullfrog . . . [and he] always had a mighty fine time . . . singing joy to the world." But that must be a different Jeremiah from the one we meet this morning. That Jeremiah talks about joy, but this Jeremiah says, "My joy is gone, grief is upon me, my heart is sick." He voices this trilogy of agony and some even suggest those words might actually be God speaking because even God suffers, right? I know that within romanticized and traditional notions of masculinity we hear that real men don't cry. Some endorse this machismo mentality. But God suffers and God weeps, even as we hear in the shortest verse of the Bible—"Jesus wept" at the tomb of Lazarus (John 11). In this passage, we have a prophet who weeps. Don't underestimate tears. They may not mean what you think, and they may come without warning.

Saint Augustine, in his *Confessions*, recounts his mother's death at the age of fifty-six, when he was thirty-three years old. He was by her side when she expired her last breath. He closed her eyes and said "a great wave of sorrow surged into [his] heart." Tears started to come but he "stemmed the flow" and the tears dried up. He thought it was more mature to put his "sobs in check" and not to mark his mother's death in that way because it was not total extinction or misery since she was a woman of faith. He fought against the wave of emotional sorrow and did not even shed a tear at the burial ground. It wasn't until he woke up the next morning that he wept for her and himself. He writes, "The tears which I have been holding back streamed down, and I let them flow as freely as they would, making of them a pillow for my heart. On them it rested . . ." His heart rests on a pillow of tears. His heart rests on grief. That same morning he was comforted by Saint Ambrose's "Evening Hymn," which declares that God will "gently soothe the careworn breast, and lull our anxious griefs to rest."[1] There's something about a mother's death that grieves the human heart, perhaps because it is the loss of our first home in the womb. In the end, Augustine could not stop his grief or his tears, though he seems to still struggle with their role in the spiritual life.

Groaning grief is often the ongoing theme in our sin-sick world. Job loss. Health crises. Deadly shootings. There's good reason for much weeping and wailing. We've seen the choreography of grief on display at vigils for those who have been killed by gun violence and even at funerals of loved ones, especially of children. Some faint in overwhelming sorrow for a young life cut too short. Others bawl like the Old Testament figure—"Rachel weeping for her children and refusing to be comforted, because they are no more" (Jer 31:15). Some swallow their tears in silent numbness at what appears to be the death of humanity's future. Some may want to jump into the casket of the child, who is no more, as an attempt to reverse life's inhumane joke that has gone sorely wrong. This grief is oral and aural and visual, choreographed by the spirit of a broken world.

We observe and hear the grief of Jeremiah. It is not a pretty sight. The pages of Scripture are soaked with sorrow and lament. He is moaning his mourning. "O that my head were a spring of water, and my eyes a fountain of tears, so that I might weep day and night for the slain of my poor people!" It is embodied grief. A grief that terrorizes the body and reshapes the contour of one's life, like when a mother discovered two children locked in a car trunk, suffocated by mistake while playing an innocent game. The choreography of grief at that moment was unforgettable! Joy was gone and her heart was sick. The terror of grief irrupted the fountain of tears from her heart. It was an observable and obvious grief.

In his personal journal, published as *A Grief Observed*, C. S. Lewis pens the shape of his grief in the wake of the death of his wife, Joy Davidman. Again, it was that c-word. Not curse word, but cancer. "Cancer and cancer and cancer," he writes. "My mother, my father, my wife. I wonder who is next in the queue." The presence of the absence was so poignant that Lewis writes, "Her absence is like the sky, spread over everything."[2] Grief

1. For the entire account of his mother's death and his own grief, see Augustine, *Confessions*, Book IX.12, 200–203.

2. Lewis, *Grief Observed*, 11–12.

takes over his life to such an extent that he declares, "I am a death's head." Somatic grief, just like Jeremiah.

Publishers Weekly notes that sales for books on grief do pretty well. There are some classics in religious circles like *A Grief Observed* or *Lament for a Son,* by Nicholas Wolterstorff. Grief sells well as people try to discover how to best deal with it. But I'm not sure the book of Jeremiah has sold as well, especially his lamentations that are found in chapters 11–20. Everybody wants to rush to prooftext Jeremiah 29:11—"For I know the plans I have for you, plans to prosper you and not to harm you, plans to give you a hope and a future." Yet, I don't know of anyone who tries to memorize at bedtime "we look for peace, but find no good, for a time of healing, but there is terror instead" (8:15). That was the state of the people in Jerusalem. I don't hear anyone quoting the lament of the people, "The harvest is past, the summer is ended, and we are not saved." Jeremiah is a weeping prophet who does not make financial profits. He does not have a bright smile or slick hair or tell funny stories. Tears are his food day and night, but his tears may not be what you think. There's something compelling, something honest, something real and raw about Jeremiah's descent into the shadow of a people's darkness. Far too long certain sectors of religion have attempted to avoid the abyss, but Jeremiah reveals the truthful necessity of facing the abyss along a trail of tears.

The prophet's oracles "indict Jerusalem for its disobedience to [God's] Torah and . . . sentence Jerusalem to the punishments that follow upon Torah disobedience."[3] His speeches anticipate the destruction of Jerusalem in an enemy assault that is the enactment of the will of a God who will not be mocked or disobeyed. It is clearly a domain of doom and destruction. This is the reason for Jeremiah's grief, joylessness, heartsickness, and mourning. The people experience a sense of abandonment and loneliness; God seems to be *in abstentia*. "Is the Lord not in Zion? Is her King not in her?" (Cf. Ps 48:3). Or in the words of C. S. Lewis, "Why is [God] so present a commander in our time of prosperity and so very absent a help in time of trouble?"[4] It is the piercing question of lamentation that God even asks God, "My God, my God, why have you forsaken me?" It is the interrogation of the biblical blues. Where is God? Old Testament scholar Stephen Breck Reid writes, "The crucible of laments is to trust in God even in the face of the apparent absence of God and the presence of the enemies."[5] Funnily enough, the people of God are not the only ones questioning. God raises

3. Brueggemann, *Introduction to the Old Testament*, 209.

4. Lewis, *Grief Observed*, 6.

5. Reid, *Listening In*, 35.

his voice, "Why have they provoked me to anger with their images, with their foreign idols?" The irony is that the Lord is in Zion and has his own questions for the people. Based on what God says, this is actually a situation of self-imposed exile and hurt based on the choices of people.

The situation is so grim that Jeremiah sings his own blues note, "Is there no balm in Gilead? Is there no physician there?" Later in the book of Jeremiah, there is restoration, but in this specific moment he doesn't distance himself from the hurt and sorrow of his people. He is not afraid to cry. "Real men don't cry," they say. But prophets do. "For the hurt of my poor people I am hurt, I mourn, and dismay has taken hold of me." His tears form a path of solidarity in suffering. Don't underestimate tears. They may not mean what you think.

The challenge is to see hope while traveling on the trail of tears. Jeremiah reveals the gift of tears, affirming what UCLA clinical professor of psychiatry Dr. Judith Orloff teaches. Professor Orloff gets excited about people crying because she has witnessed the healing power of tears. Tears are a release valve for stress and grief and anxiety and frustration and joy. Tears are a way to purge pent-up emotions so that they do not remain in the body as stress symptoms. Tears lubricate and cleanse our eyes so that they do not get irritated or infected. After crying many times, our heart rate can decrease, and we enter a calmer state. Reflex, continuous, and emotional tears make us feel better, physically and emotionally. Crying can be thought of as physiological and emotional detox through which one can be healed. Thus, Dr. Orloff warns not to hold back the tears because it is healthy to cry.[6] A Yiddish proverb says, "What soap is for the baby, tears are for the soul." Don't underestimate tears. They may not mean what you think.

There's much fruit from tears. Jeremiah reveals that they are a gift as tears embody the prophetic ministry of grief. Tears have a ministry, a prophetic ministry. It's important to remember that the office of the prophet was to ultimately be a gift for the nation as a whole. When Jeremiah cries he yearns for the restoration of his people, which is why he asks, "Why then has the health of my poor people not been restored?" As a prophet, he not only stands over against them as a mouthpiece of God, he stands with them in mourning and grief at their impending funeral. He sheds a fountain of tears as an aspect of his prophetic work.

His grief is prophetic because he refuses to be silent in the face of horror and terror and injustice. Elsewhere, he says the word is like "fire shut up in [his] bones" (20:9). He does not shrink back from voicing the raw grief of life. Prophetic grief is a form of lament that boldly proclaims,

6. Orloff, "Health Benefit of Tears."

"Life is not right!"[7] Tears can represent a torn heart, but this type of tear-filled grief can also be a form of resistance. One may shed tears because one refuses to shrink back from struggle and pain. Joy is gone but hope is not! Prophetic grief tells it like it is and acknowledges the troubles of the world. This ministry of grief is the embrace of weeping and lamentation as part of our spiritual repertoire and in the process helps others engage their experiences of suffering honestly, rather than respond with numbness, fear, self-deception, and denial of reality. Prophetic grief is poetic and can be a theological chronicle of communal catastrophe expressed lyrically. Jeremiah is not afraid to name his and his people's sorrows. Every teardrop is a prophetic act of resistance against the way life is and a prayer for something better because of his faith in God. Is there no balm in Gilead?

Prophetic grief does not leave God off the hook. It does interrogate the goodness of God. Is there no physician there? Questioning God is a part of a Christian spirituality in which we recognize that many times there are more questions than answers and it takes courage to ask God anything, especially when we may not receive the answer we want or any answer at all. But prophet Jeremiah still courageously asks questions because he believes so deeply in the loving reality of God. He doesn't ask in unbelief; he asks because he believes with deep abiding faith. He asks, "Is there no balm in Gilead?" because he does believe God is present, though he experiences theological dissonance in that he can't make sense of the hurt of his people. Yet, he hopes because there is a sense that catastrophic events do not undermine the credibility of God.

Prophets are prisoners of hope, not just bearers of bad news. Their jeers and tears are rooted in a hope in God. When Jeremiah is called (1:4–10), he's commissioned to pluck up and pull down and to build and to plant. Judgment and restoration. Warnings of doom but always followed by promises of hope. The prophetic ministry of grief is hopeful. Those who do not grieve cannot truly hope because weeping is a portal to hope. The tears flowing from Jeremiah's head are not a sign of weakness but strength of spirit in the Spirit. All of this weeping and lamentation does not represent an erosion of hope but necessary elements of hope. If one does not experience some form of grief or suffering, hope is not necessary because what are you hoping for then? In Augustinian fashion, tears form a pillow and on them, hope rests. Tears are a part of the texture of hope.

Earlier in the book of Jeremiah, we hear that God refers to himself as a "fountain of living water" (2:13) and the people use "cracked cisterns that can hold no water." Thus, this suggests that God is our living water source

7. Brueggemann, *Psalms and the Life of Faith*, 105.

and apart from him, we will be dry and thirsty. But notice, Jeremiah is full of water as his head is a spring of water, his eyes a fountain of tears. His weeping then suggests the presence of God, that God is in his tears, in the water of holy weeping. This means that hope is tear-stained. If not, it is not real hope. Tears sow the seeds of hope. These tears are sacramental not only as a sign of divine presence but as a sign of our own baptism, the waters of the Spirit's washing. So God is in our tears.

In what became his last book, *The Scandalous Gospel of Jesus*, Peter Gomes, the former Pusey Minister at Harvard's Memorial Church, reminds us that "Hope . . . is not the opposite of suffering; suffering is the necessary antecedent of hope," because in and through suffering, hope manifests. "A hope worth having, is forged upon the anvil of adversity . . . Hope is the stuff that gets us through and beyond when the worst that can happen happens." He writes, "Hope is not merely the optimistic view that somehow everything will turn out all right in the end if everyone just does as we do. Hope is the more rugged, the more muscular view that even if things don't turn out all right and aren't all right, we endure through and beyond the times that disappoint or threaten or destroy us."[8]

In other words, as Durham's own Pauli Murray has said, "Hope is a song in a weary throat."[9] Or, as the pastor emeritus of Allen Temple Baptist Church in Oakland, California, J. Alfred Smith, has proclaimed, "hope is a tiny sprout growing in cracked concrete."[10] That means the tears, the suffering, the weary throat, the cracked concrete, are the settings out of which hope is born. Hope comes amid our grief, despite our grief, but not without it. Hope is tinged with the ashes of despair and hope resides in the ruins, even in the demonic milieu of historical human slavery.

It is still so mind-boggling to me that the gift of the spirituals was given in the bosom of inhumane slavery. That, as James Weldon Johnson pens, "The fiery spirit of the seer should call these simple children of the sun and soil." That though these black slave singers were "gone, forgot, unfamed, untaught, unknown, unnamed," their songs "still live" and touch the chords of our human hearts today.[11] That when we find ourselves in the home of grief and declare "my heart is sick," at such times as school massacres, we turn to a spiritual like "Balm in Gilead" to grieve and hope at the same time. This music created in the womb of melancholic misery straightens out Jeremiah's question and turns it into an exclamation point. There is a balm in Gilead!

8. Gomes, *Scandalous Gospel of Jesus*, 311, 307–8, 306–7.

9. Murray, "'Dark Testament.'"

10. Smith, "Foundations of Our Faith," 143.

11. Johnson, "O Black and Unknown Bards."

A note of triumph in the midst of any type of terror. Not happiness. Not joy. But hope.

Jeremiah's sorrowful wounds did not win nor did the wounds of God destroy God. Rather, his cruciform wounds, his tear drops of blood, were the balm for the healing of the world, including our own. There is a balm in Gilead to make the wounded whole.

"The balm in Gilead [may be] the spiritual itself."[12] A song. A melody. A tear. Don't underestimate tears because they may not mean what you think. They may reveal that you are actually a prophet and those who sow in tears will reap in hope. And hope, according to poet Emily Dickinson,

> is the thing with feathers
> That perches in the soul
> And sings the tune without the words
> And never stops at all.[13]

Questions about the Question

- What current situation needs a balm to be applied to a wound?
- Why is it difficult to have hope?
- How do you experience tears?

12. Troeger, *Wonder Reborn*, 47.
13. Dickinson, "Hope is the thing with feathers."

10

Why are you afraid?
(Mark 4:35–41)

Jesus can really, really preach. He doesn't pastor a megachurch or host a Christian TV talk show. He hasn't written any *New York Times* best-selling self-help books and he doesn't even ask for an honorarium when he preaches. He just comes to Galilee to do ministry, proclaiming the good news of God that "the time is fulfilled and the kingdom of God has come near; repent and believe in the good news." Mark wants us to know that Jesus came preaching. And boy can he preach! I know preachers get a bad rap in today's society with the litany of scandals and they are, Fred Craddock tells us, "as one without authority."[1] But from the beginning, Mark doesn't pay attention to the media, and frames the ministry of Jesus with a focus on preaching. Jesus came preaching and he even says that he came to "proclaim the message." And what a message—the kingdom of God has come near.

I wish Jesus was my preaching professor in seminary. He has a way of integrating his talk and his walk. He does what he says. His word takes on flesh because he is the Word made flesh. We don't need to read philosopher J. L. Austin's William James Harvard lectures, *How to Do Things with Words*, to recognize that Jesus is a divine Word that does something. His word calls and people follow. His word teaches and it has authority like no other preacher's. His word exorcizes unclean spirits. His word heals the sick, even the paralyzed. His word cleanses lepers and heals withered hands.

1. Craddock, *As One Without Authority.*

His proclamation of the good news of God includes words and deeds. His preaching realizes that which it proclaims! Jesus is the real deal.

He won't ask you to send in $19.95 before he sends you a prayer cloth. He won't ask you to donate online via PayPal. His powerful gospel is free, and his homiletical rhetoric matches his ministerial ethic. What a preacher. He lives the sermon, and his words do something in our lives. Even speaking parables by the sea is not enough for him because "on that [same] day" in the evening, he gets into a boat with his disciples on the sea to show them how he does things with words. There is a Markan shift from the words of the parables to his works in the world. Here on the sea, we have what has been called the first of the four mighty acts. His words take on flesh again. They do something on the sea. Rather, they do something to the sea.

But not everyone understands what Jesus does through his proclamation. Everyone won't understand every single sermon that is preached. Some may respond with an affirming "amen!" But there will be others who respond with an "Oh my!" That's the case here with the preaching of Jesus. Don't just pay attention to his words but watch the actions that occur through words because when he acts, he's proclaiming too! Jesus and the disciples are on a boundary-crossing mission and that in and of itself can be stormy. They are on the sea, a symbolic context of chaos. A "great windstorm arose, and the waves beat into the boat, so that the boat was already being swamped." A natural storm was raging, beating them down in the boat, while a quiet spiritual storm was brewing in the disciples' hearts. They think they are about to drown, and Jesus is calmly sleeping as a sign of trust in God. He's asleep yet alive to God. The disciples are awake but numb to God, like sleepy Christian zombies. Even after Jesus wakes up, rebukes the wind, silences the sea, ceases the wind, and there is a dead calm, we still hear the chaotic storm raging in the disciples' lives. In the silence of the sea, if you listen closely, we can hear the beating of the fearful hearts of the disciples.

Jesus just proclaimed "Peace! Be Still" and it happened—the natural storm ceased. Read the CNN headline news—"Jesus Christ Superstar, does it again." But the disciples are freakin' out with fear and faithlessness. "Why are you afraid? Have you still no faith?" Jesus does not beat around the bush. He cuts to the heart of the matter, to their hearts, to do spiritual surgery. The trouble is not the storm because storms are inevitable. The winds and the waves of a turbulent world will come. The trouble is the fear of the disciples even after the calm, the miracle, comes. The dead calm does not change their living fear. Perhaps they are, as New Testament scholar Brian Blount says, "afraid of the calm."[2] Maybe the calm makes them crazy because they're

2. Blount and Charles, *Preaching Mark in Two Voices*, 73.

used to chaos and the storm is the norm. I don't know, but what I do know is that after this powerful preachment, the disciples should at least be doing the happy dance or the Holy Ghost shout or the electric side or the boogie woogie, or the hokey pokey, or the limbo, or the funky chicken. Rather, they "get jiggy wit it" and do the jittery jig of fear. They feed on fear for spiritual food. Why are you afraid? Jesus is near, but they still have fear.

Their fear is a sign of a weak faith and even an absence of faith. The presence of the absence of faith due to fear is stronger than the real presence of the kingdom of God in their midst, right in their little boat. Fear blinds them to God's presence and creates a deficiency in their theological epistemology, so they ask, "Who then is this, that even the wind and the sea obey him?" The disciples don't get it even after Jesus explains everything in private to them and tells them the mystery of the kingdom of God. The disciples don't recognize him but in Mark, the demons do! The kingdom of God is as near as the flesh of Jesus Christ in the boat, but the disciples still have to ask, "Who is this?" The demonic sea understood more than the disciples. They sleep on God's presence and need a great awakening. Fear has blinded them, and they can't see the theological reality right in front of their eyes. They're afraid because they don't know who Jesus is. They may wear nice shiny crosses around their necks, attend church and Sunday school weekly, engage in social justice ministry, pray at bedtime and over meals, lead Bible studies and mission trips, and sing in the church choir, but Jesus still has to ask, "Why are you afraid? Have you still no faith?"

Those questions come echoing down the acoustical corridors of biblical history to us. Why are you afraid? The proclamation of Jesus is not always easy to handle. Those probing questions are a challenge to us. Do we really trust God in the midst of the storms of life that rock our boats? Because, our faith is tested in the storms, when our sailboats are being swamped, and like the psalmist we declare the water is up to our necks. Our faith is not tested when life's computer has not crashed, and all is well. Our faith is tested at the bottom of the pit of hell or in a boat being beaten by winds and waves. If we're not careful our fear may drown us and our faith in the sea of despair.

Fear will limit the boundaries of our call to discipleship. Fear is antithetical to faith, which is why Jesus asks, "Why are you afraid? Have you still no faith?" Fear has nothing to do with trust in God. The issue is not if the storm will come, but when. The lightning will flash, and the thunder will roll. The winds will blow, and the waves will crash while waters try to flood our lives. The real issue is our response to the wet weather. The real issue is the "fear factor." Why are you afraid in tough times, in the face of great obstacles? Do you only have what John Wesley called a "dry land, fair weather faith"? Have you no faith because it suffers from seasickness on the stormy seas of fear?

Fear of economic uncertainty in the future. Fear of future political leadership in the world. Fear of the other, difference, changing demographics, so much so we get into our bunkers to "protect borders." Fear of not knowing what is to come. Fear of being out of control. Fear of the cancer returning. Fear of an abusive spouse returning. Fear of not being loved. Fear of dying alone. Fear of a failure and even fear of success. Why are you afraid? At the heart of the plethora of fears is a fear of the apparent absence of God when in fact God is near in Jesus. Why are you afraid? Only you truly know why. But it may be from not knowing who Jesus really is. "Who then is this, that even the wind and the sea obey him?" Time after time, Jesus is present in the world and in our lives, but we still question, "Who is this?" How can we trust someone whose presence we don't even recognize in our lifeboat?

In the aftermath of the horrendous 2010 earthquake in Haiti, there was a Haitian man who was trapped under a slab of concrete from a collapsed building. He lay on his side as the weight of this piece of concrete rested on top of him. All of this was caught on camera. A news reporter was right there, ready to get high ratings. This reporter conducted an interview with this man as he lay on his side underneath a slab of cement, and this is what she asked—"What are you telling yourself?" Well, hmm . . . what do you think he's telling himself as a cement block rests on top of his body, squeezing the life out of him? "I forgot to put out the garbage this morning? Oh shucks, I didn't respond to that email?" "What are you telling yourself?!" This man should have said "I'm asking myself why a news reporter is interviewing me right now?" Or, he could have uttered angry lament from his lips: "My God, my God, why have you forsaken me?" But instead, in response to the reporter's question, "what are you telling yourself?" and in response to the sea of rubble all around him and on top of him, he says "Jesus, Jesus, my life is in your hands." Under the weight of a broken slab of cement, under the weight of the world, comes a profound statement of trust and faith. He knew who Jesus was during his crushing storm. His life, his security, was in the hands of Christ, come what may.

This is where the disciples miss it, and they wonder who this is who has just calmed the seas. They fear and have no faith, yet their deliverance from the storm still happens. The prosperity, name-it-and-claim-it preachers would not like this story because the disciples lack faith, but God still acts on their behalf. They have feeble faith, but God in Jesus Christ is faithful. Despite our fear and lack of faith, Jesus stills the stormy seas and brings peace. Jesus does not operate according to the adequacy of our faith. God's activity is not dependent on whether we have faith or not. God's activity is dependent on God. Jesus works according to the way of the kingdom of God. Jesus is the kingdom of God in the flesh, and he has power over creation. Jesus does kingdom work even when we don't understand, when we fear and when we have no faith. Jesus does not wait for us to try to figure him out. Jesus does not wait for us to sign the dotted line to go on a mission trip. Jesus ministers with or without us. Jesus eventually goes to the other side of the sea to fulfill his boundary-crossing mission, to still another storm. If Jesus waited on us to act, he might never act. The good news is that we can't stop the ministry of Jesus!

Our fears will not stop the kingdom of God coming near. Jesus will not be fenced in by our fear. We may not recognize him, but God is always at work. God intervenes in human history through the proclamation of Jesus. God is loosed in the world through Jesus as the heavens are torn apart at his baptism. Jesus is not just sitting in Starbucks drinking a nonfat caramel macchiato with whip, waiting for us to act in faith. Jesus is not in a virtual internet church world, waiting for us to sign in online to worship. Jesus is in the real world. And Jesus can really, really preach. Jesus is present and not just present but active, not just in our boats but in the world.

So when he crosses to the other side of the sea and gets out of the boat, he casts out an unclean spirit from a man who had been tormented by the tombs. He stills that storm and, in the end, makes that man a preacher. Who then is this? Jesus, the Lord over any chaos. His words do things. And when he speaks, even your storms will have to listen.

Questions about the Question

- What storms do you see brewing in the world?
- What are you afraid of?
- Why do we not always recognize the presence of Jesus?

11

How can this be since I am a virgin?
(Luke 1:34–55)

My father once told me to take a song with me on the journey of life. I take not only a song with me, but this particular story with me wherever I go, because young girls have their special way of truth-telling. In the fall of 2006, some of the children from the Dupree Center for Children, the preschool of Princeton Theological Seminary, participated in the daily chapel service. There was a livelier buzz than usual in the frozen chosen Reformed liturgical tradition's air on this day. For that service, I was asked to lead the congregational singing of a hymn, the spiritual, "Guide My Feet." I was happy to do this and thought it would be cool for my daughter Moriah, who was four years old at the time, to see Daddy in action. I came up front in Miller Chapel and took my place. As I led that hymn, Moriah stood in the front row staring at me, not singing a lick. No lips-moving, no smile-making, no eye-winking, just a numb stare. I knew she could get easily embarrassed by me in public by what she considered to be my lack of wardrobe sophistication. But that wasn't it this time. Knowing Moriah, I thought her countenance in the service was pretty strange for her personality. I couldn't wait to get home to ask her about it. So when I got home, the first thing I did was to ask her, "What did you think about Daddy's singing today, sweetie?" She said something I'll never forget, "You sing like the Cookie Monster."

Yes, the Cookie Monster. The one on Sesame Street. The one with blue fur and googly eyes. The one who says, "Me want cookie." That one. Young girls have their special way of truth-telling. Pavarotti, Michael Jackson, Paul

Robeson, Sting, Johnny Cash, even Dolly Parton, but the Cookie Monster?! In the movie *Forrest Gump*, Forrest was right: "Life is like a box of chocolates; you never know what you're gonna get." I didn't know what I was gonna get on that day.

And Mary had no clue what she was gonna get from the angel of God. Let's just say that Mary didn't jump up and down as if she'd just won the Holy Ghost lottery when the angel told her that she was going to give birth to God's Son. Maybe the angel thought this was going to be good news. But that's not how it was received. In today's world when one hears "the Lord is with you" or "you have found favor with God," there may be a hand raised in praise, a loud amen, or at least the Presbyterian amen. But Mary does no such thing. She's perplexed and has a hermeneutics of suspicion, questioning what it all means. She says to the angel, "How can this be since I am a virgin?" Mary is not in a singing mood unless it's the blues. But we can't blame her, can we?

Our perception of her as *theotokos*, the holy mother of God, the virgin mother, may place her in a sanitized heavenly, spiritual realm at a distance from our human situation. But remember Mary is an engaged teenage girl who just found out she's having a baby and not from her fiancée, Joseph, a man with royal blood working on Wall Street. She's pregnant before she even gets married. Can you imagine the gossip spreading at the coffee hour after worship? If it wasn't bad enough to be in a society where a woman needed a man to be worth anything, now this happens? As she receives those words from the angel, I can hear her catch a lump in her throat. "How can this be since I am a virgin?" How can this be? Haven't we asked that before? How can this be happening in my life? It's unbelievable.

Mary struggles and I'm not sure when and what makes Mary shift while she waits—whether it's receiving the news about her once barren cousin Elizabeth's conception or hearing that "nothing will be impossible with God"—but Mary transitions from "how can this be?" to "let it be." "Let it be with me according to your word," as she waits for the divine promise to be fulfilled in her life. This young girl is betwixt and between, in a liminal space between yesterday's promise and tomorrow's fulfillment of that promise. It's a time of uncertainty and anxiety, a time of being unsure about the future of this country, a time of being unsure about the future of the church as we know it, a time of being unsure about the future of your current life situation, whatever that might be, betwixt and between, a season of waiting to see if God will still make a way. And as she waits, it may surprise you to see what Mary does. Mary begins to sing and that starts a revolution of redemption as God overturns our expectations in the tough circumstances of life and does the unexpected through the form of a song.

What do you do in seasons of waiting and transition when the future is unknown? Mary could have done many things while waiting for the promise to be fulfilled—she could have put her head in the sand, pouted, doubted, shouted in desperation, thrown herself a pity party, indulged in overeating, overdosed on pills, read Karl Barth's *Church Dogmatics* or one of the volumes of *Chicken Soup for the Soul*. She could have yelled out for help and lifted her voice in despair, Cookie Monster style—"Me want help!" Instead, God lifts up a hymn through this teenage girl to let us know that singing is still possible and preferable in these kinds of predicaments. To many, singing is a royal waste of time. But young girls have their special way of truth-telling—to sing in the midst of unsure times, to sing while you wait for God to do something, to sing at these moments is the ministry of "prisoners of hope." As we've heard oft-quoted—"hope is a song in a weary throat."[1] And Mary's situation is no different, revealing how at transitional and uncertain periods in life, singing is an art form that will take you from one place to the next as you migrate with God. It's true for Mary and true for us. We sing as we journey because one thing is for sure, music is portable ministry and bearers of God sing.

So Mary holds one of the world's greatest hymn sings. What Mary does by singing a hymn is a revolutionary way of living the Christian life and responding to uncertainty. To sing a hymn when life sucks. That's the challenge. To sing a hymn to God when you're not even sure you trust God with your life anymore. That's the challenge. To sing a hymn when you're in the waiting room of life not sure what the future holds. That's the challenge. To sing a hymn when you discover a loved one or friend has been diagnosed with cancer. That's the challenge. To sing a hymn when it seems as if the tune of hate is the societal melody of the day. That's the challenge. To sing when all is well and life's computer has not crashed is not a challenge. The courageous miracle is to sing a hymn when all hell is breaking loose, and it seems as if all you have is the song itself. Mary's anxious lump in her throat becomes a song. Mary was maybe weary from worry but hope still makes a melody in her heart that crescendos through her voice, and we hear it echoing as the *Magnificat* down the acoustical corridors of church history.

This ancient hymn is not what was expected in these circumstances and functions as a song of resistance to cynicism, negativity, and hopelessness. Mary is not out of touch with the reality of her situation because she sings. That she sings demonstrates she's in touch with a Reality greater than her own life. She's in touch with God and sings to reach out to God in order to transcend the difficult circumstances of her life. She is a kind of caged

1. Murray, "'Dark Testament.'"

bird of sorts but her song, her hymn, is a sign of her freedom even amid uncertainty and liminality.

Our wings may be clipped. Our feet tied. But as long as we can open our throats to sing, we are free and alive. Mary doesn't allow the unknown to hem her in; rather, she trusts God enough to raise a hymn when those around her may think it's insane to do so. She doesn't have all the answers or understand everything that's happening but "[she] doesn't sing because [she] has all the answers; [she] sings because [she] has a song."[2]

And as appropriate with a hymn, this song is about God, not Rudolph the red-nosed reindeer or seeing Mommy kissing Santa Claus underneath the mistletoe last night. "My soul magnifies the Lord, and my spirit rejoices in God my Savior, for he has looked with favor on the lowliness of his servant . . . for the Mighty One has done great things for me, and holy is his name. His mercy is for those who fear him from generation to generation." God is the theme of this song. God is in this song. That's why hope sings. That's why this hymn is still being sung all over the world generation after generation. Because "God has shown strength with his arm. God has scattered the proud in the thoughts of their hearts. God has brought down the powerful from their thrones and lifted up the lowly; God has filled the hungry with good things and sent the rich away empty. God has helped his servant Israel."

Christian hope magnifies God in the middle of anxiety and uncertainty. Church music has a God focus and rightly so and this intoned hope anticipates the future through hymn sings. Mary sings the future of God and when she sings, she starts a revolution because as Bernice Johnson Reagon of Sweet Honey in the Rock reminds us, "You can't sing and not change your condition." As she sings, she prepares the world for the entry of the incarnate Hope it needs. As she sings, she declares that the world is about to turn and in fact, an eschatological reversal has already begun even with the virgin birth itself. God doesn't come as a king on a white horse or cruisin' in a flashy Mercedes Benz. God comes in the form of a baby. This hymn foreshadows God's overturning of human expectations. For what is up will come down and what is down and low will be brought up and put on high. The empty will be filled, and the full will be emptied. God will turn our world upside down and it happens even as we sing. Worlds crumble in the face of singing doxology.

A hymn will rock and revolutionize your Christian faith and the world because this is God's song. How do I know this? Who else could it be that would use the art form of a song to usher God's hope into the world? Who

2. Anglund, *Cup of Sun*, 15.

else could it be to use a teenage girl from an insignificant village to give birth to God? Who else would lead you to sing amid earthquake rubble?

Of all the things that one could do when a 2010 earthquake destroys a country like Haiti, singing is not necessarily at the top of the list. So it was incredible to see and hear our brothers and sisters in Haiti singing on the streets day, noon, and night. This was not the expected response to catastrophe. Of course, there was crying and screaming and groaning and moaning, but there was also lots of singing. Ena Zizi, a seventy-year-old woman, had been buried for a week in earthquake rubble that was at least three stories high from the ground. When she was pulled out of the rubble, she was seriously dehydrated, and had a broken leg and dislocated hip. But that didn't stop her. When they pulled her out of the rubble, this lady began to sing. Her body was worn and her throat was weary, but hope was singing.

Let songs of faith rise out of the rubbles of your existence even as you wait for God's intervention. They sang in Haiti because they were still alive, and their singing meant that God was still at work somehow somewhere. Their songs were an invocation for God to intervene and their songs indicated that God had already come, and God was in the song.

God isn't finished with us yet. Their singing, our singing, Mary's singing, all say that Death will not play the final musical postlude, which is why we continue to sing during this interlude waiting period of life. It doesn't matter what you sound like or if you think you have a good voice or not. It doesn't matter if you have a weary throat that can't hold a note. It doesn't matter even if you sing like the Cookie Monster. I'd rather be a Cookie Monster for Christ than a divo for the devil.

Begin your Cookie Monster ministry and sing like the Cookie Monster because he's unashamed in front of other people. Sing like the Cookie Monster because his voice is raw and rugged, which shows us that he knows something about struggle in life. Sing like the Cookie Monster because we don't know what Mary sounded like or if she was a soprano, alto, tenor, or bass, but we do know she sang in the tune of God and others leaped for joy. For all we know, she might've sounded like the Cookie Monster. And remember the early church adage: "he who sings, prays twice."

Lift every voice and sing. O for a thousand tongues to sing. How can I keep from singing? I can't keep from singing. Let's have a hymn sing!

> I'm gonna sing when the Spirit says sing
> I'm gonna sing when the Spirit says sing
> I'm gonna sing when the Spirit says sing
> And obey the Spirit of the Lord.

Questions about the Question

- When have you been in disbelief about something?
- How do you handle uncertainty?
- What is the role of song in your life?

12

What is your name?

(Luke 8:26–39)

We are on the brink of healing, but we can't seem to get there as a people or as a nation. It seems as if we're always on the brink like a broken record stuck on the same musical line. We continue to run endlessly on the treadmill of terror. We never quite reach the place of healing. We want healing, don't we? Or, maybe we don't. Maybe we can tell what we really want and who we really are by our name.

There's something about a name, the meaning of a name, the way it rolls or doesn't roll off your lips. A name you cherish or one you've changed for various reasons. Your name. It means something. If it didn't, some people wouldn't decide to use their middle name instead of their first name or choose a new name altogether or keep their last name or use a hyphenated name when they get married. There's something about a name.

Cameron means "crooked nose." Kennedy means "ugly head." Brian means "maggot." Caleb means "dog." Portia means "pig." You have to be careful with names.

Today we encounter some names, one name in particular you probably would never want to be called. Nobody prays for this one and the main protagonist in our story didn't either. We don't know how he got the name, but we can surely see how this name shapes his life. And what a name it is—Legion.

When Legion is your name you might think your parents were stoned or drunk at a frat party when they named you, or they were playing a bad

April Fool's joke. He's stuck with this name like Krazy Glue—Legion is like a leech. This isn't a name that recruits followers. It wasn't his fault, your fault, that you were called this. It wasn't as if you prayed the rosary or wrote it down in your journal as a bucket list plea. It just happened one day. Your name was Legion, out of nowhere. And Legion refers to a Roman army of four to six thousand soldiers. That's one problem for every soldier. This is a big name with a big impact on this man. It's so devastating it shreds him to pieces, shredding every piece of cloth off his body. He's naked. He rents a residence among the tombs. He's tormented. Legion. A name, this six-letter name, means something.

Legion is not a nice name for anyone because it means he was driven by demons into the wilds of a tortured territory. It means that sometimes we are full of sickness, possessed by vast powers other than God. Tormented. And the irony is that we, or our sickness, love the name Legion, love the torment, love tombs as tents because a storm is the norm for us; it is our usual reality and we know nothing else, so we love it because we love what we know, even if it hurts us.

We can be so ill that when a healing opportunity stares at us face-to-face in Jesus we beg not to be tormented—"I beg you do not torment me!"—when in fact all we've known has been torment and trials and terror. Legion was on the brink of healing before his healer, but the illness is that the torment brings comfort and safety when it may be killing him. We just don't recognize it. Ironically, when Legion is your name, calm and serenity are a threat when they should be a relief. Abuse makes you feel good. "I beg you do not torment me!" Some who are sick don't want to be healed.

And to go even further, when this man, possessed by demons, is clothed and in his right mind, it's at that point that the people become afraid. The same thing happens when the disciples are on the boat in a storm—when Jesus brings calm, then they become afraid. What's wrong with us? It's true, even if we don't want to admit it, that some people love chaos, love trouble, love torment, always invoking problems into their lives. We can be on the brink of healing and not really want it. Legion knows no other way of life or being. This is especially true when one has been tortured one's whole life, or at least for a part of it, to such an extent that what's normal becomes normative. Healing doesn't even look like healing anymore. Life doesn't look like life anymore.

We see the result of having Legion as a name. Animal rights activists may get perturbed over this, but we see the trajectory of a legion-filled life. What happens to the swine when the demons enter them is the end result of a tormented life. "The herd rushed down the steep bank into the lake and was drowned." This is the end when spirits other than God possesses one.

This is the end when one's name is Legion. Living and dying among tombs, keeping funeral homes in business.

So, what is your name today? I don't mean your given birth name or baptismal name. The man who lived among the tombs was up front about his name and his predicament. It was Legion. But what is your name?

People are not always that straightforward about their identity. But I'm reminded of a Maya Angelou saying, "When people show you who they are, believe them."[1] We can discern some people's names by their actions. "Hi, my name is Joy." But why are you always so negative? "My name is Peace." So why are you always stirring up conflict? Jesus doesn't actually ask other people in this story for their name, only the possessed man. But we can read others' reactions as the script of their lives, therefore their lives tell us what their names are. When the people came out to see what had happened and when they came to Jesus, "they found the man from whom the demons had gone sitting at the feet of Jesus, clothed and in his right mind. And they were afraid." This man whom they knew as the crazy Gerasene or "crazy Gery" in their neighborhood. This man who ran wild, naked and breaking chains, was now healed. But unlike a later story of a lost son, these people don't celebrate or cook a fatted calf. No parties for this one who has indeed returned to himself. Rather, they ask Jesus to leave them "for they were seized with great fear." What is their name? These people reveal that their name is "Fear," and it shapes their whole life.

On the brink of healing, they are afraid of healing and the healer. They ask Jesus, the healer, to leave them. The one they actually need, they want to get rid of. Perhaps the demon-possessed man wasn't the only one sick in this story because they are sick too, so sick they fear wholeness and calm, so sick they fear a resolution to gun violence. They fear change because the healing of this man who is now clothed and in his right mind would be an alteration in how they treat him and relate to him. They don't see his healing as a benefit for them.

Healing affects everyone, all of our relationships, not just the one healed. That's why some prefer slopping it up with swine rather than seeing their fellow human beings saved. That's why it's so easy to keep things the way they are—to say nothing about gun violence or to remain silent about hatred toward those who are different in any way. It's so easy to do so when we aren't the ones naked or running wild among the tombs, when we aren't the ones ostracized in society or the ones whose sanctuaries have been desacralized.

1. Podrazik, "Oprah's Life Lesson From Maya Angelou."

The truth is that some of us don't want to be healed nor do we want others to be healed because it will change how we have to relate to others and ourselves. Healing will change our reality and the bottom line is that many don't like change even if it's the best thing for everyone. We like the way things are and the way things have always been done and we never question it.

> A little girl noticed that every time her mother cooked a roast, she chopped a piece off the end of the roast before putting it in the oven. She asked her mom why she did this. "Well to be honest, I do it because that's the way my mother always does it . . . I'm sure she must have some good reason for it." At the next family gathering, the child decided to satisfy her curiosity. "Grandma, why do you always chop the end off the roast before cooking it?" "Well to be honest, I do it because that's the way my mother always does it . . . I'm sure she must have some good reason for it." A week or so later the little girl was visiting her ninety-year-old great grandmother. She explained that her mother and grandmother always chop the end off the roast before cooking it, but couldn't remember why. Did she know? Great grandma replied, "Imagine the two of them doing that! I only cut the piece off because my pan was too small!"[2]

We like what we've only and always known and nothing more, even when it comes to the possibility of healing, even if it means someone remains sick. Fear can set in on the brink of healing because in these Gerasene situations, we only know how to talk to Legion. We don't know how to talk with someone whose name is "healer" or "healed." When Legion is gone we may feel that we've lost our best friend or the life we've always known. Therefore, the breakthrough for another person, the freedom for another person, the healing and restoration of another, might be experienced as a loss for us, though it's a gain for that person. No wonder we ask Jesus to leave—we don't want anything to change because we know when Jesus is present everything has to change.

This is what happens when your name is "Fear" on the brink of healing, and if this is the sad truth, then we may not always have each other's best interests in mind because we can receive a healing as a loss, a seismic unwanted change, so what do we do? We fear the unknown, altered, healed future, not thinking of what is best for those who've been naked, tormented all their lives and tenting among the tombs. We can't trust each other for our healing, especially not when you're dealing with names like "Legion"

2. "Pan."

or "Fear." We may actually like those names because it's normal. "Mass shooting in Orlando" is normal. "Killing people in a Bible study at Mother Emanuel AME church in Charleston" is normal. "Massacre of the Innocents at Sandy Hook elementary school in Newtown, Connecticut" is normal.

The status quo of violence against and hatred of the other is deceptively, comfortably normal. How it's always been is too easy and can be used as a way to keep Jesus out of the way. The legion of xenophobia and the legion of gun violence are too lovable for many, more adored than fellow human beings, which is why we tell Jesus to take a hike. We ask him to leave our lives, our county, our country, even when we witness a demon-possessed man becoming a disciple, even when we see tortured life transformed. There's no rejoicing in this healing. We fear it. That's the real sickness—apathetic social status quo under the veneer of a so-called Christianity. It's sick when tombs are a hot sale in the human home market and we are fine with it. That means we are more satisfied with torture than healing.

We may not want Jesus around because we not only fear what healing means for our lives but also fear that he may ask us the same question he posed to Legion—"What is your name?"—and we fear what our answer may be. We don't want to hear the truth or face the truth of our own reality.

If I were to ask you what your name is, what would it be? Legion? Fear? Anger? Frustration? Lonely? Depression? Lost? Confused? Stating your name, naming your struggle or problem, naming what you are full of, is a step toward your healing, a step toward your freedom, a move toward being clothed and in your right mind. So, claim your name today just like Legion did. He had to name his torment to open the gateway to healing. Name it because if you don't, you won't be set free from your inhumanity. Name it because if you never name it, it will never be cast out. Like at Alcoholics Anonymous meetings, someone will stand and say, "My name is . . . And I'm an alcoholic." They name their struggle as part of the healing process.

You may still be trying to figure out your real name, not what others call you nor what you pretend to be. You may not know your name right now, but you do know that you are tormented and in need of healing. Regardless of what your name might be, it's critical to turn to the One whose name is above every name. It's key to turn to Jesus on the brink of healing and not tell him to go away; that would be horrible timing. His name, at which every knee will bow and every tongue confess, is the name we need to call. Jesus, there's something about that name. His name is mentioned more than Legion because his name is more powerful than any other name. His name is the source of healing not only in this story but also in the ones that follow as he heals two women—Jairus's daughter and a woman hemorrhaging blood. Built into his very name is what he does.

Names mean something. When he is born, we hear that his name will be called "Jesus" for he will save his people from their sins (Matt 1:21). He will save. He will heal. Jesus, the sweetest name on earth. Jesus, lover of my soul. Jesus, healer of the nations. "All Hail the power of Jesus' name, let angels prostrate fall, bring forth the royal diadem and crown him lord of all." He may be asking you what is your name and knowing your name is critical, but he wants to be sure that you know his name.

A life shaped by his name means that your wounds will become a source of healing. You will have scars but that just means you've been healed. If you don't have scars, you're either not human, have never been hurt, or you're not healed. The real sign of being healed is going away and acting on that healing and sharing it with others. It's never just to sit with Jesus as Jesus sends the healed man away from him to preach. We must act on our healing and we surely need healing agents of God, now. We are on the brink of healing—and many are right that praying isn't enough—it's time to act. In Jesus's name.

Questions about the Question

- What do your given names mean?
- Have you been called other names? What are they?
- What name do you want Jesus to call you?

13

Will he find faith on earth?

(Luke 18:1–8)

When the Son of Man comes, will he find Faith on earth? I ask because Faith is on the verge of needing a heart transplant. She's had a couple of heart attacks and almost died in church one Sunday morning after the choir sang an arrangement of the Rolling Stones' "I Can't Get No Satisfaction." Her heart is still pumping, but for some reason the blood is not flowing like it once did. The doctors are saying that the pace of her heart is becoming too slow. Faith has been through so much in such a short period of time. She's had a couple of bypass surgeries but that doesn't seem to have been a huge help. Faith has lost some of the weight that she was carrying around but she is still moving sluggishly. She's tried all kinds of heart medications but that hasn't been much better. Now, the doctors are talking about the possibility of a pacemaker, but she doesn't like that idea. Faith is beginning to lose heart and she's getting tired. If her heart's health isn't bad enough news, her insurance company is threatening not to cover her any longer. You can't blame her for being down. She's on the verge of giving up. And many times, she's by herself in the hospital because the family of Faith rarely stops by anymore to encourage her.

Faith was the mother of the church. She fed so many in the church family, especially during those lunches in the church basement after the Sunday morning service. But there she is now, Faith, alone, *sola fide*, lying on the bed of despair, still trying some of those well-worn spiritual therapies like saying the Lord's Prayer over and over again, especially that line about "do not bring us to the time of trial," even though she feels like she's being put on trial. That prayer doesn't seem to work anymore. She's even gone back to her childhood days and tried "now I lay me down to sleep, I pray oh Lord my soul to keep. If I should die . . ." But she can't get past that part—"if I should die." She's having a hard time finishing any of her prayers these days. Faith barely prays anymore because she doesn't know how to pray anymore and nothing seems to heal her heart. None of her prayers seem to be answered—in the silence, the only answer she hears is the echo of her own voice. You can prooftext all you want—"ask, and it will be given you; search, and you will find; knock, and the door will be opened for you." You can prooftext that all day long in your congregations but Faith knows from experience that one can ask, search, and knock, and not receive, find, and have any doors opened.

The heart of Faith is failing and I'm wondering, "When the Son of Man comes, will he find Faith on earth?" Things are not looking good for Faith. When the family of Faith does visit her, they sometimes read Scripture to her to lift her mood. The other day, they chose to read Luke 17:22 to 18:1–5. Faith was having a pretty good day until her family started to read those texts. Words about judgment, suffering, rejection, corpses, death, and a widow who needs justice. Light subjects. This is not necessarily the best kind of theological bedside reading for pastoral care of those suffering from heartache and pain. You don't have to enroll in seminary to know this. For heaven's sake, what was her family thinking when they chose these passages? The context for this reading is even the death of Jesus, for Jesus is on the way to Jerusalem, the place of his death, the place where he leaves the earth, and leaves others confused and grieving. The family should have done their exegesis before they chose these texts. Faith didn't want to hear about death and Jesus leaving earth. She wanted to know that Jesus is on earth and can fix her broken heart. Were they trying to kill Faith and send her to an early grave? Were they really trying to make her feel better and soothe her heart with words like "The days are coming when you will long to see one of the days of the Son of Man, and you will not see it"? The lightning will flash and light up the sky from one side to the other. "But first he must endure much suffering and be rejected by this generation." The days of the Son of Man will be like the days of Noah and Lot. Those were the "happy days" all right. And then one woman will be taken, the other left and where should we find her? "Where the corpse is, there the vultures will gather." Vultures having communion on corpses. I'm sure that encouraged Faith. That was really good news. What were they thinking? These words of Scripture are not for the fainthearted but they read them to Faith anyway, even though they know she has a hurting heart. Their presence, or at least those readings, didn't make her feel any better. It only made things worse. She grew even more fainthearted.

Even the story about the widow, the outsider in society, the one who had all the odds against her, yet fought for justice and got the justice she sought, was not a comfort to Faith. It was a challenge to her. She couldn't handle it right now. Rather than being an encouragement to her, the widow was a discouragement. She felt like she failed and fumbled as a Christian. She didn't pray always. She wasn't like this persistent widow. She had lost the fight in her and was on the verge of losing her heart. She couldn't take any more uncertainty and anxiety in her life; her health condition was enough. This eschatologically driven uncertainty in the setting of this passage was too much for her. Even the disciples don't really get it when Jesus talks to them and foretells his death and resurrection. "They understood nothing about all these things; in fact, what he said was hidden from them, and they did not grasp what was said." His very own disciples. No wonder Jesus tells them to pray always and not lose heart or faint because he knows their trust in him would be tested in the uncertain times in which they lived. Pray always and don't lose heart? Jesus tells the disciples to pray always and not lose heart because they are losing heart and fainting into a deep spiritual sleep. These same disciples are the ones who are found by Jesus sleeping because of grief on the Mount of Olives. Pray always and not lose heart? Yeah, right. Does Jesus really know what it's like to follow him? The disciples were on the verge of becoming fainthearted on the journey, just like Faith. We can't blame them. We can't blame Faith for struggling with the weight of the world's circumstances and things unseen. About the only thing she sees is unanswered prayers. What does the future hold for Faith?

If it was up to us, Faith might have been dead a long time ago. I know the doctors changed her diet, but look at what we fed her to clog her arteries of belief. No wonder she has heart problems now. Some ecclesial camps fed her the misconception that if you name it and claim it, you'll get it from God—this became the "word of Faith" for a while. She was naming and claiming but God seemed to be refusing to answer, at least in her timeline. God was like the unjust judge and she was the widow who was wearing him out, hitting him under the eye, boxing God for a blessing. But I've never known God to lose a battle. She fought hard for health and wealth and prosperity but only realized more disparities between her and others who questioned Faith. Faith was learning about the Christian journey but we didn't help the situation by feeding her discouragement because we didn't tell her that God can be silent and slow in answering our prayers. We never fed her the truth that delay was the order of the day many times. That might have cleared up her arteries. We never told her about the reality that praying meant waiting unlike those who approach prayer like rubbing a genie lamp to make a wish to receive whatever is desired. Faith was not smiling and there were no answers to her questions. Why did my child die from cancer? Why was a little girl killed, perhaps by her very own mother, then buried with a heart sticker on duct tape covering her mouth? Why did my spouse cheat on me? Why can't I get pregnant? Why did I lose my job? Why do I feel so alone? Why aren't you answering my prayers, God? Why is my heart failing? My God, my God, why have you forsaken me?

I don't know. When the Son of Man comes, will he find Faith on earth? That's the question of the hour for the family of Faith. When you do your daily routine and life is tough and you see a discouraged Faith again lying on her bed of despair with her bleeding heart because of unanswered prayers, what then? Will he find Faith on earth? The other questions in this passage have definitive answers. Will not God grant justice to his chosen ones? Yes. Will he delay long in helping them? No. But, will he find Faith on earth? Maybe? I know he'll find us worrying about our 401Ks and retirement pensions. I know he may find us still bickering over denominational dogma and social issues. But will he find Faith on earth? Faith has always been the one who has made us well, as she did with the ten lepers. Faith has been the one who has always saved us, as with the blind beggar by the side of the road. But now Faith is no longer able to be the caretaker, the pastor. Faith is the one in need of pastoral care and you know how hard it is to pastor pastors! What happens when the heart of Faith begins to lose its blood? What happens when Faith, our Faith, gets tired? We can't lose Faith now. If it was up to us, Faith might be dead because of what we fed her. But it's not up to us.

It's up to God. For even during these trying times, as she lays flat on her back on the bed of despair, Faith has to look up. Our Faith. Sometimes I call her "my faith." Now, "My Faith looks up to thee, thou Lamb of Calvary, Savior divine!"[1] Is this the same Faith? How is this possible after all she's been through?

When the family of Faith left the other day, they left Faith a green Gideon's Bible. Her heart was fainting but the eyes of Faith still worked so she decided to open up to the passage they read to her. And she realized that they forgot to read what Jesus promises after he tells the parable about the widow and the judge. She began to read aloud and though the arteries of the heart of Faith were clogged, she could still hear the Word of God, the promises of Jesus Christ. And despite her struggles, and despite lying flat on her back, Faith was standing on the promises of Christ, his word, not the word of faith, but the Word of God. And as she read the Word, it was

1. Palmer, "My Faith Looks Up To Thee."

as if the Word read her life, the Word was speaking to her heart, making promises only he could keep.

To her, this was the most important part of the passage: "Listen to what the unjust judge says. And will not God grant justice to his chosen ones who cry to him day and night? Will he delay long in helping them? I tell you, he will quickly grant justice to them." This made all the difference to Faith because the emphasis is on the unjust judge's eventual yielding to the widow's persistent plea, not on the widow herself. Jesus basically preaches the bad guy here, the unjust judge, and not the widow. He doesn't say watch her, follow her, imitate her. He says, "Listen to the judge." Jesus stresses the giving of justice, the Giver of Justice, a giving God. If an unjust judge will give justice and answer pleas, how much more will a just God give justice and answer prayers? Like any good sermon, Jesus has one sermonic theme about prayer—it's not us, but God. Will not God grant justice? Will God delay? God will quickly grant justice. God will do right by you—that's justice. God will right what is wrong.

Faith is learning that God will do right by her despite her circumstances. Faith is learning that prayer is all about God. Faith is learning that the sustenance of the Christian life is dependent on God, not on Faith. Faith is turning her attention to a caring God and away from her health predicament. Faith is recognizing that she doesn't have to lose heart anymore when she doesn't get the answers she wants when she wants, because she realizes that prayer is about a God who will eventually answer her call, a God who will do right by her, a God who will give her justice, a God who will eventually come to her aid. Faith is beginning to see that prayer is about not seeing God and not seeing answers but still believing in a God you cannot see, trusting God's mighty acts throughout history, trusting that "God don't never change" and God is good all the time and is always on time. Faith even thinks that this pericope shouldn't be called the "parable of the persistent widow" but instead the parable of a persistent God—that's the point Jesus makes—a God who's always willing to grant justice and give answers, despite a fainthearted Faith. That's what Jesus promises to Faith. And we know God fulfills God's promises. But Faith abides between a loving promise and hope for its fulfillment. All Faith has is a word of promise and Faith is taking God's promises to heart.

I really don't think we're going to lose Faith now. Faith is still in bed, wearied from life's storms, and not fully recovered; I don't think she'll ever be perfect. But Faith is standing firm on the promises of God and this word is starting to pump some new life and blood back into her heart. This word is spiritual medicine for her soul. She can't do much activity right now but she's starting to pray again because Faith without doing any kind of work would be dead. She wants to be active and prayer has become what John Calvin calls the "chief exercise of faith."[2] But she knows that her life is not totally dependent on her, Faith, but dependent on the Word of promise. Faith knows that sometimes all we have is a promise, a Word, but this Word is not any kind of word, but a Word, once God speaks it, that will not come back void. A Word that does something, and we don't need speech-act theorists to tell us this. A Word that creates something out of nothing. A Word that is sent and heals our diseases. A Word that can just speak and someone be made whole. A Word that stills storms. This Word does something. This Word promises "I will not forget you." This Word promises Faith "I will give you a new heart." And this Word of promise goes all the way to Jerusalem, to give blood on a cross in order to keep the heart of Faith beating. This Word started the Red Cross to fulfill his promise. And Faith is so grateful. You can tell by her heartbeat. Do you hear it?

Questions about the Question

- How would you assess your faith right now?
- What gets in the way of faith?
- What gives you faith?

2. See Calvin, *Institutes of the Christian Religion*, Book III.XX.1.

14

Why are you weeping?

(John 20:1–18)

Mary Magdalene has forgotten that it is Easter. According to one writer, there are three essential prayers—help, thanks, and wow.[1] Easter is supposed to be a wow day. Right? But Mary makes it a woe-is-me day instead. Come on, Mary, don't rain on our Easter parade and dampen the mood. Don't wrinkle our frilly dresses or mess up our fancy new hairdos or crush our favorite white lilies. O Mary, don't you weep. But that's exactly what she does "early on the first day of the week, while it was still dark." Mary "stood weeping outside the tomb" in a pool of tears that drench this story. The pages of the pericope are still seemingly moist with Good Friday sorrow. It is trumpet-tongued, brass-blasting Easter! Yet Mary reveals that we can be an Easter people living in a Good Friday world. Mary "stood weeping outside the tomb." Weeping is more than tears; it includes wailing and lamentation for the dead. It's an ancient Jewish expression of mourning and grief.

Why does Mary weep? She says, "They have taken away my Lord and I do not know where they have laid him." Mary does not weep as a sign of the penitence of the gift of tears nor does she weep over the bitter division in this country over human equality. Mary weeps because she mourns the loss of Jesus. The God she knew is gone. She did not mourn the death of Jesus in this case, because Jesus was already dead. She weeps because Jesus

1. Lamott, *Help, Thanks, Wow.*

is lost. The One who declared his ministry major to be finding the lost, was lost himself, and she couldn't find him. Her weeping, or what John Donne calls "fruits of much grief,"[2] flows because of the presence of the absence of Jesus. Jesus is MIA, missing in action. Mary had gone to the tomb because that was where she was used to finding Jesus, the dead Jesus, the impotent Jesus, the Jesus-who-does-not-meddle-in-my-life Jesus, comfortable and cozy Jesus. Mary had become used to the place of death. She weeps because what she had come to expect had shifted all of sudden and everything she knew, Jesus, was gone. She weeps due to a nostalgic disorientation.

"They have taken away my Lord, and I do not know where they have laid him." Mary still expects to find a dead Jesus in a dark tomb, located in the same old place and acting in the same old way. Controlled, cold, numb, and locked in a grave cave. Mary has forgotten that it is Easter. She weeps because she has lost what she has known to be reality, the usual place where she thought she could find Jesus forever—in a mausoleum manger. "They have taken away *my* Lord," my personal Jesus, my concept of who Jesus is. I wish I could return to the days when it was as simple as "Jesus is the answer," a simpler way, no complexity to theology, no unanswered questions because the "Bible tells me so," the good old days when I ruled God from the throne of my own anxiety, and wrapped an entombed Jesus, not in swaddling clothes, but in a psychological safety blanket. That dead Jesus was gone for Mary. Where she left him, he could no longer be found. The Jesus she knew and believed in was lost, the tame Jesus of her childhood, the one with blond hair, blue eyes, and a pointy nose on the fans used in the country church. Her Jesus, her Lord, was lost. The one she understood. The dead Jesus laying in a dead place.

This is in stark contrast to what Anne Lamott dreams about in her book *Plan B: Further Thoughts on Faith*. She dreams of an Easter like the resurrection vision of a child in Sunday school who drew an Easter Bunny, not Mary, outside of the empty tomb, joining eternal life with a basket full of chocolate eggs. With that vision, the tomb would be tasty—yummy, yummy to my tummy. What an Easter it would be—chocolate, white chocolate with macadamia nuts, dark chocolate melted over strawberries, Hershey chocolate ice cream cake, chocolate-covered grits with scrambled eggs. Maybe or maybe not. Either way, scientists have argued for years how eating sweet chocolate makes us feel good and is more pleasurable than listening to your favorite music or winning the lottery or even falling in love. Chocolate can lift you to heights you've never seen before, they say.

2. Donne, "Valediction of Weeping."

Lamott dreams of a chocolaty Easter—innocent, childlike, and carefree, full of chocolate fountains flowing deep and wide outside of the tomb with the Easter bunny as the doorman. This is a dream, not the reality she knows. On the contrary, she's not surprised by Mary's weeping in a Good Friday world.

Mary, not the Easter bunny, stood outside the tomb, without a basket full of chocolate eggs, but carrying despair and hope in the chest of her heart. Mary weeps because she finds herself in a Good Friday predicament on Easter morning. What else can she do in this situation? She could post a jazzy and flashy neon-colored flyer with Jesus's picture on it and put "Missing" at the top and hang it outside of the local grocery store. But how could she do that when it seems as if Mary doesn't even know what Jesus looks like anymore? She had lost Jesus, or at least her conception of him. She had gotten so used to a dead Jesus that a living Jesus was a stranger to her. And how strange this is when Mary learns how to weep from Jesus who wept at the tomb of Lazarus. She picks up where he left off—weeping. Mary loves Jesus and her tears are signs of that grieving love. But maybe the flood of tears blinds her eyes so she doesn't recognize Jesus when Jesus asks her face-to-face, "Woman, why are you weeping? Whom are you looking for?" She "saw Jesus standing there, but she did not know that it was Jesus." She sees him but doesn't see him with the eyes of faith. You can love someone but once that person changes you may not recognize them anymore. They may be so different because death and life are different. A dead Jesus is distinct from a living Jesus. Jesus had changed clothes because he was alive and shook off the sting of death's designer attire. Death's clothing won't fit on a living God. Jesus left his tomb linen suit in the deathbed of the grave and was now wearing living clothes of light.

The question "Whom are you looking for?" suggests that the real issue was that Mary was looking for the wrong Jesus, a powerless dead Jesus in a cold tomb, just lying there. Not a living risen Jesus and Lord. She doesn't recognize him because she wasn't used to a living risen Jesus. She looked for him in the wrong places and had gotten used to a God who lies dead, inactive. A small, lifeless Jesus she could control and even carry around as she offers to take him away, if she can find out where he lays. But the living Jesus looks right at her.

Then Comedy Central arrives in the midst of a tragic time. After Jesus asks her why she's weeping and who she's looking for, Mary speaks to him "supposing him to be the gardener." She's talking to the incarnate God but thinks he's a gardener. That's like walking around in a department store shopping and someone asks you if you know what row the Clorox bleach is on—and you weren't even wearing an employee name tag. What made

Mary think that Jesus was a gardener? Was it his tattered clothes or his accent or his humble demeanor, or his skin color or his body odor? Was it that he resembled God in the garden of Eden? Was it the sweat on his brow or the scars on his hands? A gardener? You can't always judge a book by its cover. The writer of Hebrews teaches us not to neglect showing hospitality to strangers because by doing so some have entertained angels without knowing it. Mary was entertaining the resurrected God but she didn't know it. She saw a gardener.

According to various accounts, Sir Winston Churchill did not have the greatest relationship with his parents. As a young boy, he was berated by his father and told that he would grow up to be a failure. They perceived him to be less than what he was. What they saw, he was not. On top of that, he had a speech impediment and was discouraged by some of his teachers. Sadly, most of us have probably had a teacher or a school counselor like that, who only knew how to be a midwife for stillborn hope. Yet, Churchill became one of the major twentieth-century leaders in the world. You can't judge a book by its cover. Too small. Too big. Too tall. Too short. Too thick. Too thin. Too loud. Too soft. Too uneducated. Too unsophisticated. Too human to be divine.

Jesus can be right in front of us but we don't recognize him because we think he's just a yard maintenance man. Our lack of recognition keeps us weeping in the dark of dawn. Even when resurrection comes, we may not recognize it because we've become so used to, so familiar with crucifixions, dying, and death. And as the psychologists have taught, familiarity breeds liking. Liking death can become the norm when we hold membership at the Jerusalem temple of the tomb. Those who attend services there are dead, too, among the saintly zombies or at least counting down to the date of their death on the website deathclock.com. No wonder weeping occurs. That is, weeping over our own death. Perhaps Mary weeps because a part of her dies when Jesus died. I don't know, but I do know that she weeps because of disorientation due to losing her Jesus, the dead Jesus. But she's the one who's really lost because she doesn't know resurrection when it's even staring her in the face.

Good Friday weeping on Easter intrigues me, but I guess it makes sense since my former students at Princeton Seminary used to call me "Dr. Death." Mary's weeping is fascinating and I wonder something else about her weeping. Unwittingly perhaps, Mary weeps even as a deep yearning for the return of Christ. In fact, she weeps for resurrection and as a summons, an invocation for the presence of the risen Lord. She doesn't know this but her tears are prayers. Sometimes we cry and we don't even know why. We're weeping for resurrection. Jesus wept for life over death, and we weep for life over death. In this context, we are reminded of the words of Jesus, "I am the resurrection and the life"(John 11:25).

Jesus, the one who rises and calls us by name ("Mary!") even if we don't recognize him, even if we think he's still dead, is calling you. The risen, living Jesus refuses to be imprisoned in death's solitary confinement. This living Jesus cannot be controlled by our theological paradigms or ecclesial traditions embalmed in a tomb. We won't find the living Lord of light there, dressed in death's dingy clothes. Jesus is alive and on the move in the world, which is why he tells Mary, "Do not hold on to me." You can't control me. You can't hold me down or hold me back or keep me dead and useless. There's too much work to do in the world. Too much interceding and healing and comforting and reconciling. Bringing peace in the midst of conflict. Love where there is hatred. Justice where there is oppression. "Do not hold on to me" with your sanctified straitjacket. Release me for the work of redemption. To ascend to the Father in order to lift you higher. Don't look for me at the tomb. You'll look for me and I'll be gone. I'm not there. I won't bring you back to the way it was because I'm no longer dead. "The way out of the darkness is only by moving ahead"[3] into my resurrection light. Don't dwell on the memories of the past, but remember the future I have for you.

Why are you weeping? Mary weeps not because she fears death but because she fears life, the new, adventurous, unpredictable, resurrected life and future in Christ. The old, lost, dead, predictable, comfortable ways, dead Jesus, had passed away. Behold, the living Jesus was making all things new. Weeping for all things new. A new start, a new beginning, a new day, when there would be no more tragedy and agony. All things new. What we see in the flesh of the risen Lord is God's embodied promise that a new day has begun in Christ and that resurrections still happen. All things new. A new start with your family that had fallen apart. A new job when you've just lost a job. A new dream for your life when you thought all you were capable of were nightmares. A new medical invention that may actually help cure cancer. All things new.

Because Jesus got up, we can get up, as he lifts us up as he ascends to the Father. Mary was down but when Jesus calls her name he lifts her spirit up, he wakes her up, he resurrects her, which is why she had been weeping for resurrection all along. Mary hoped for all things new. Mary's weeping ceases in the presence of the resurrected Christ, who resurrects her when he calls her name. She was dead but in that moment he made her alive. She no longer needed a dead Jesus because the living One was right in front of her.

3. Barnes, "Savior at Large."

Mary had "seen the Lord" and her life was never the same again. She became an apostle to the apostles.

After all she had been through in the past, this was an unexpected future. We can't control the future but Christ leads us into the future and holds the future. We can't hold on to him because he's actually holding us. Why are you weeping? O Mary don't you weep, mothers don't you weep, fathers don't you weep, sons don't you weep, daughters don't you weep, students don't you weep, faculty don't you weep, facility workers don't you weep, coaches don't you weep, university administrators and staff don't you weep. Because in the life of the risen Christ we pass from death to life, from death's tomb to God's triumph, from an old age to the inauguration of a new one. An age when "[God] will wipe every tear from [our] eyes." An age when "death will be no more; mourning and crying and pain will be no more." An age when we just might have chocolate for breakfast, lunch, and dinner.

Mary had forgotten Easter in her Good Friday world. But she no longer weeps and we no longer have to sing, "O Mary don't you weep." For weeping may endure for the night but Easter joy comes in the morning. Jesus is not dead. He is alive. It is a wow day. Christ is risen. He is risen indeed. Not even an Easter bunny chocolate can beat that. Alleluia!

Questions about the Question

- Why are you weeping?
- What gets in the way of seeing the Lord right in front of you?
- What does the resurrection mean to you?

15

Do you not know that you are God's temple?

(1 Cor 3:10–23)

Right before the beginning of this 1 Corinthians lesson, Paul says, "We are God's servants, working together; you are God's field, God's building." Then in this lesson, he says, "you are God's temple." God's. You are God's. If you only heard me say that sentence orally, it could be taken in two ways: you are gods or you are God's. That apostrophe in the latter version makes a huge difference. Of course, there's no apostrophe in the Greek grammar but there is the genitive case, the possessive—God's. God is a genitive God and in English, it's indicated by the apostrophe. That little punctuation mark makes all the difference, theologically.

But not everyone has been happy with the apostrophe throughout history. In 2010, an article written in the *MIT Technology Review* made that clear. Supposedly, "grammatical tragedy struck" Birmingham, England, where the city council declared that apostrophes were to be banned from public addresses. So "St. Paul's Square" would become apostrophe-free and be "St. Pauls Square." This council believed that people in general didn't understand how to use apostrophes appropriately on public signs and "they were a hindrance to effective navigation." For example, stories were told of ambulance drivers trying to figure out how to input "St. James's Street" into a GPS while victims of heart attacks and other ailments suffered and died because of it.[1]

Apostrophes do reveal possession but also indicate a missing letter, as in the contraction "it's." Moreover, when words are in plural form and end in an "s," how do you write the possessive form of that plural word? Is it the toys' color or the toys's color? Pronouns don't even use possessive apostrophes—we don't say, "I's paper" or "me's shoe." And to go even further, on a computer keyboard, the apostrophe is the same key as the single quotation mark. Apostrophes can be confusing. Knowing how and when to use an apostrophe isn't always easy.

Yet despite all of the misunderstandings around apostrophes, it is our saving grace because we learn that we are God's. God's servants, God's field, God's building, God's temple. We are possessed. Some may not like that language of possession and wish we would remove that apostrophe, which would then give a totally different meaning with the sentence "we are gods." But I will say this—that if you are not God's, you are someone or something else's. You belong to something or someone, even if it isn't God. It might be Paul or Cephas or Apollos. Someone or something possesses you. Some are possessed by jobs and overworking hours to the detriment of a healthy life. Some are possessed by alcohol or other addictions. Some are consumed by the Internet or social media and not able to break its trance over them. You are possessed, but by what or whom?

There are competing loyalties ad infinitum, even as we see in the Corinthian church. And even if you remove that apostrophe in "God's," and consider yourself to be gods, then you are in possession of your own life, apart from God. You are possessor. Removing that little punctuation stroke is a way of saying that you don't need God and will only relate to your own gods. We then are self-possessed. To be gods, sans apostrophe, is how human beings got into trouble in the first place with the tower of Babel. "Come, let us build ourselves a city, and a tower with its top in the heavens, and let us make a name for ourselves" (Gen 11:4). But God confused them and scattered them all over the earth. Why? They forgot that they were God's; they ignored the apostrophe. But I say, "Thank God for the apostrophe." How about that for a testimony? Tell your English teachers that I was grateful for apostrophes!

There is saving grace in that one small punctuation mark. One small alteration—inclusion or exclusion of it—can change the meaning and direction of your life. Removing the apostrophe will cause you to lose your soul because you won't be God's; you'll only be gods. Leave the apostrophe in.

1. "Curious Case of the Evolving Apostrophe."

It changes everything. You are God's. It changes whose we are and who we are. God's.

I realize that talking about the gift of an apostrophe is not as titillating as the latest TMZ gossip in the Corinthian church newsletter or in the White House these days. There's so much to inquire about and of course inquiring minds want to know. Want to know about who's really in charge and whether Paul has true authority, want to know about pending lawsuits, and sexual immorality, and riotous behavior at the Lord's Supper, and class struggles and wiretaps, and leaked emails. This is the stuff that gets high ratings, even in congregations! But this isn't breaking news, although I do have some news. Good news. All because of that apostrophe in Paul's letter. You are God's, God's temple, and what a privilege it is.

"Do you not know that you are God's temple and that God's Spirit dwells in you? . . . For God's temple is holy, and you are that temple." The temple in Jerusalem was still standing as Paul writes this. That temple was the visible center, the dwelling place, of God's presence. Today, we may even think that grand cathedrals or places of worship house God, but they don't because God houses us and hosts us in life. No building, no structure can house God's holy presence. And Paul, by telling the people—you are God's temple—makes the courageous shift by emphasizing that God's presence dwells among the collective body of the people of God. "You are that temple" is not a reference to individual bodies (though he teaches about this later in the letter); rather, he speaks to the community of faith as a whole in their life together. In the new revised southern version of the Bible, Paul declares, "Y'all, you all, are God's temple and . . . God's Spirit dwells in y'all." He addresses the "you" plural. He addresses us. "Y'all are that temple." The faithful community of believers. The church as a temple of the living God.

The apostrophe makes the theological difference. You are God's temple. You are God's holy dwelling place. It means we are possessed, Spirit-possessed. An embodied spirit possession is not the only way to be possessed by God. As the body of Christ, God's Spirit dwells in you, thus you are Spirit-possessed. "God's temple is holy, and you are that temple," like it or not. Being possessed by God, being God's, doesn't make you perfect. Clearly it doesn't; just look at the crazy Corinthians and all of their tensions. Observe today's Christians and you know we aren't perfect, especially if you consider some of our church bulletin mistakes: "The peacemaking meeting has been cancelled due to a conflict"; "The sermon this morning—Jesus Walks on Water. The sermon tonight—Searching for Jesus"; "Potluck supper at 5 PM. Prayer and medication to follow."

The church is imperfect and being possessed by God may not make you perfect, but it does make you holy because holiness is not dependent on us, it is dependent on God who is holy. The church at Corinth is holy because God's Spirit dwells in them. And the same is true for us as Christ's followers. Holiness is not something we possess or create but a gift given by God in Christ through the Holy Spirit. Holiness is based on a holy God and we are a temple because of God's presence. If *the* Real Presence is not present, we have no temple status.

But you are that holy temple and what a privilege it is. In the Bible, to be holy means to be set apart for the service of the holy God. Again, it comes back to that apostrophe that signifies possession. You are holy as a people because you house the Holy Spirit of God as God's temple. You are holy, not "you are perfect." You are holy, housing heavenly treasure in earthen vessels. You are holy means you are possessed by God, cherished by God, desired by God, trusted by God. You are entrusted with God's presence. You are loved by the One who is love. When others see flaws and scars in a community like Corinth, God sees your scars as confirmation that you are a part of God's family in Christ, because Christ knew about scars. It seems to be the family trademark. James Weldon Johnson penned:

> Jesus, my lamb-like Jesus,
> Shivering as the nails go through his hands;
> Jesus, my lamb-like Jesus,
> Shivering as the nails go through his feet.
> Jesus, my darling Jesus,
> Groaning as the Roman spear plunged in his side;
> Jesus, my darling Jesus,
> Groaning as the blood came spurting from his wound.
> Oh, look how they done my Jesus.[2]

A holy Christian community will be a scarred community; this is definitely true if Christ is the foundation of this temple, and he is. As the hymn says, "The church's one foundation is Jesus Christ, her Lord . . ." The church is rooted in the ministry of Jesus Christ. Out of this Christian theology, ethic, and ethos, we serve. It's the recognition that God gives the growth. We may plant. We may water. But God gives the growth. That's why it's all God's. As one commentator notes, the substructure of the temple is provided by Christ and the superstructure by human beings. We aren't holy. We are made holy. We aren't gods. We are God's.

And housing the holy, being God's, is more than a turn inward to the divine treasure within and among us. Being stewards of the holy presence has to do with turning away. The Greek linguistic roots of "apostrophe" mean to "turn away." That holy punctuation mark in "God's," the genitive form, is

2. Johnson, *God's Trombones*, 42.

a "turn away" from ourselves, away from sitting on our own thrones, away from boasting, away from having our own way, but toward Jesus, toward God's way, toward others. To be God's is to be for those in the world God loves. When you are God's, there's always a centrifugal force propelling you away from the self toward and outward on the mission of Christ. Being God's temple, housing the Holy Spirit, has an ethical import.

We may handle holy or sacred objects with such delicate care but how do we handle the holy people of God, the human community of Christ who is the temple of the Spirit? How does the holiness of a human being or a human community call us to a certain relational ethic in which we affirm the sacredness of every human life? The problem with the Corinthian church, the problem with us, Christians, at times, is that we forget the primacy of love because we forget whose we are. We forget the apostrophe. We can have all the spiritual powers and exquisite gifts on display, yet if we act without love, it's just noise, and we hurt the holy witness of the community. If we truly believe that we are caretakers of the holy as God's temple, this should result in better behavior in word and deed toward one another. Knowledge puffs up. Love builds up. "Let all things be done for building up," Paul says (1 Cor 14). Love doesn't tear down others, no matter how strongly you disagree with them, because if you tear down those who tear down, you become the very thing you abhor. But the way of love is God's way and it builds up. It builds the temple of God. It builds the church. Love is the criterion of all Christian action. It is not a feeling or attitude but actions of costly service towards others. It is a turning away in order to turn toward because love is for the common good when you are God's temple.

> One cold winter day a 10-year-old boy was standing barefoot in front of a shoe store, looking through the window, and shivering in the cold. A lady approached the boy and asked him what he was doing. "I was asking God to give me a pair of shoes," the boy replied. The lady took him by the hand and went into the store, and asked the clerk to get a half dozen pairs of socks for the boy. She then asked if he could give her a basin of water and a towel. He quickly brought them to her. She took the boy to the back of the store, knelt down, washed his little feet, and dried them with a towel. By this time the clerk had returned with the socks. Placing a pair upon the boy's feet, this woman then purchased him a pair of shoes, and tying up the remaining pairs of socks, gave them to him. She patted him on the head and said, "You feel more comfortable now, don't you?" As she turned to go, the surprised boy caught her by the hand, and looking up in her

> face, with tears in his eyes, answered the question with his own question: "Are you God's wife?"[3]

She wasn't God's wife but she was God's and that apostrophe made all the difference in her life and someone else's life. I thank God for little things. Little babies born in Bethlehem, little congregations who house the vast presence of God. A little piece of bread and little sip of wine that reminds us of the firm foundation of this holy temple at the Lord's table. That apostrophe makes all the difference and it's our saving grace today. Long live the apostrophe.

Questions about the Question

- Who or what possesses you?
- Why do we forget the apostrophe in "God's"?
- What does being God's temple mean for you in daily life?

3. "Are You God's Wife?"

3

WHAT SHOULD WE DO?

16

What shall I cry?

(Isa 40:1–11)

Like many other biblical questions, another true question is raised by the prophet Isaiah. "What shall I cry?" We live that question often. What shall I cry when there are thousands of deaths due to a global pandemic? What shall I cry in the face of the devastating rise in unemployment and the anticipated economic fallout from a coronavirus? What shall I cry in the face of this reality? Is the vaccine going to work? What shall I cry? "I'm tired of wearing masks, weary of social distancing and hand sanitizing, and being afraid of an unseen virus." What shall I cry? "I yearn to be hugged again. I'm lonely, isolated, and desire to gather in groups and see faces without masks. Can't things just get back to normal?" What shall I cry?

There are so many things to cry out about. And we can't make sense of what to cry out because of all of the many voices speaking and crying out, telling us what to cry out about. Very much like this Bible passage, there is often a crazy cacophony of cries racing through the tunnels of our ears, minds, and hearts, in the morning, throughout the day, in the middle of the night when we can't sleep. We may be hearing voices crying out for justice for those who have been unlawfully killed and imprisoned. We may hear voices crying out for vote recounts. There are voices crying out with conspiracy theories about political elections and mysterious viruses. There are voices saying wear a mask, don't wear a mask, get this type of mask, cloth mask, plastic mask, designer mask, this mask works, that one doesn't work, cover your nose, wear it like this, your nose isn't covered, put it on now, take it off now, wear a mask, distance six feet, you're not six feet, and wash your hands like this.

It can be so confusing to discern among the voices you hear what voices to really listen to and then determine what you should say, if anything. What shall I cry in this moment? We live this question.

There was a similar problem in Isaiah. There were so many voices speaking so that it's hard to make sense of who's actually speaking and who's saying what and when. Everyone was getting a word in at a time of Babylonian exile. God's people had been devastated, ransacked, hurt, placed at a huge distance from home, made strangers in a foreign land, serving a term to pay for their penalty of sin. And at the turning point when we learn that the exile will be ending, which begins with Isaiah 40, multiple voices speak into the situation. The first voice is God's. "Comfort, O comfort my people . . . Speak tenderly to Jerusalem and cry to her that she has served her term, that her penalty is paid." The next voice cries out, "In the wilderness prepare the way of the Lord, make straight in the desert a highway for our God." Then another voice says, "Cry out!" Then the next voice rings out in response, "What shall I cry?" Then a voice continues with the recitation about grass and fading flowers and tells Jerusalem to bring good tidings and proclaim, "Here is your God."

There are at least five voices crying out in eleven verses! Among so many voices and perspectives on the ancient Near Eastern cable television network, it can be difficult to know what to cry out and what to say at such times. What shall I cry, especially when everyone else seems to have something to say? Aren't there enough voices speaking already? Please don't offer another careless conspiracy theory. We need the truth, even about ourselves. What shall I cry?

The truth is, "I" am grass. We are grass. The people are grass. The grass withers. The flower fades. Maybe a healthy and honest sense of self is what's needed first in order to cry out anything. What shall I cry? Well first, let's recognize who we are in the grand scheme of things, in our grassiness, our finitude, our frailty, compared to the breath and Word of the Lord. As grass, all I can do is cry. All I can do is raise questions because I am not the answer. I am not God. I am a fading flower in the field, withering grass in the forest. A pandemic or bodily aches and pains remind us of our fleeting mortal nature. Put it on your tombstone and tell the truth—"I was grass."

This voice of truth is not doom and gloom and despair but actually a portal to God's presence. When you know you are grass, when you see yourself for who you truly are, this is an indication that you've encountered God. A truthful assessment of oneself tells me you are standing in the light of the truth of God. We recognize who we are when we are with God when

God is present. This is what happens to Isaiah when he has the vision of God in the temple. When he encounters God, that is when he says, "Woe is me! I am lost, for I am a man of unclean lips"(Isa 6). In other words, I am grass.

Knowing that we are going to fade, to die, should shape how we live, including our speech. If you are a flower fading, what do you want to do and say with this one life on earth? What speech habits do you want to cultivate? What good news or good tidings can you offer the world? Even grass is given the gift of sharing some good news. From this humble, lowly posture, close to the ground, one is ready to speak, not of self, but of God. The grass withers and the flowers fade but the Word of our God will stand forever. What shall I cry? Or better, *who* shall I cry?

Jerusalem, Zion, is told to lift up their voice with a megaphone on the mountaintops with good tidings and proclaim, "Here is your God." God is the good news. God is coming. God is the heart of proclamation. God in your mouth, in your vibrating vocal cords, in your piercing cry in the wilderness. Speak of God, O Jerusalem, speak of God, church, because this is the good news. The good news is God news. Dietrich Bonhoeffer once said in a sermon that people are more interested in going to movie theaters and sporting events than the church, because the church talks more about trivial things than God. I thank my *doktorvater*, Paul Scott Wilson, of the University of Toronto, who made a deliberate turn to God in his scholarship and stressed that God should be the center of sermons, the center of our homiletical cries.[1] If anything should be on our lips, it is the phrase, "Here is your God." The church is a theological entity. God should be on our lips, the Word of God in our mouths, because it is what lasts. It is forever. We don't last as grass. God and God's word are eternal, so why not offer the good gift of God to those around us?

There are good tidings to share even at such a devastating time in human history. These are the times in which God thrives. The songwriter put it this way: "Got any rivers you think are uncrossable? Got any mountains you cannot tunnel through? God specializes in things thought impossible. God will do for you what no other power can do." According to Isaiah, there is good news, a good word, even for those who've been suffering a long ways from home, even in the face of all that we see happening around us. The good word is a God word. The Word of God about God.

What shall I cry as a believer, not a political pundit, but as a follower of Christ? What message will be on your tongue?

"Here is your God." This is what we should cry. "Here is your God." There are many voices clamoring for our attention in this moment of

1. For example, see his *Setting Words on Fire*.

history. But I haven't heard many people speaking of God. God won't win high media ratings, but we aren't after high ratings in the church, as far as I know. We are after faithfulness. We are after the truth, the truth that is God.

And what God's people hear in Isaiah is that their long midnight of exilic suffering is going to turn into an eternal day. The joyful proclamation is that they, that we, haven't been abandoned forever. Here is your God. God doesn't forget us even in tough times. God has come. God is here. God is coming. I know it's been hard. I know it's been long. I know we want to get back to "normal" to a place of rest and comfort and peace and familiarity, away from all of the turmoil and angst and bitterness and fear, get back to the good old days.

But don't miss God's presence among all the tweets. Here is your God, coming with might and strength, feeding the flock like a shepherd, gathering the lambs in his arms, carrying them in his bosom, gently leading them home. God, both strong and gentle, is the only One who can ultimately deliver us, even when we've been lost and don't know what to say. "God specializes in things thought impossible. God will do for you what no other power can do."

What shall I cry? God. God is coming. God seeks us out, even as we question. God wants to be with us and will caress and carry us home. But when God comes, it may not look like what we expect and God may come in a form we never imagined—a highway in a desert, a valley lifted up, mountains made low, crooked ways straightened out, rough places smoothed, a mighty warrior as a tender mother. God comes but may do so in unexpected ways, which is why we may miss God among us.

You might have heard about a religious man who was once caught in rising floodwaters. He climbed up on the roof of his house and trusted God to rescue him. A neighbor came by in a canoe and said, "The waters will soon be above your house. Hop in and we'll paddle to safety."

"No, thanks," replied the religious man. "I've prayed to God and I'm sure he will save me."

A short time later the police came by in a boat. "The waters will soon be above your house. Hop in and we'll take you to safety."

"No, thanks," replied the religious man. "I've prayed to God and I'm sure he will save me."

A short time later a rescue services helicopter hovered overhead, let down a rope ladder and said, "The waters will soon be above your house. Climb the ladder and we'll fly you to safety."

"No, thanks," replied the religious man. "I've prayed to God and I'm sure he will save me."

All this time, the floodwaters continued to rise, until soon they reached above the roof and the religious man drowned. When he arrived in heaven, he demanded an audience with God. Ushered into God's throne room, he said, "Lord, why am I here in heaven? I prayed for you to save me, I trusted you to save me from that flood."

"Yes, you did, my child," replied the Lord. "And I sent you a canoe, a boat, and a helicopter. But you never got in."

Get into God. "Here is your God," rescuing and delivering you. Do you have eyes to see and ears to hear?

For when God comes, God also cries out among all of the many voices. And remember, it's the Word of our God that will stand forever, not anyone else's. And when God speaks nothing is left the same. All things are made new and transformed by an eternal Word—deserts, valleys, mountains, uneven ground, rough places, and people. In your wilderness, terror will be transformed into glory because the mouth of the Lord has spoken.

And what does God cry to those in exile who we never hear speak at all? What does God cry even if you don't cry? A double portion of comfort for all the craziness. "Comfort, O comfort, my people." Or as fourteenth-century mystic Julian of Norwich said, during her own experience of a pandemic, "All shall be well, and all shall be well, and all manner of thing shall be well."[2] Live the questions, but never forget, God is the ultimate answer.

Questions about the Question

- What is there to cry out about now?
- What hinders your cries?
- How do you discern God's voice among other voices?

2. See Julian of Norwich, *Revelations of Divine Love.*

17

Have you never read?

(Matt 21:33–45)

I probed the hidden depths of my soul and wrung its pitiful secrets from it, and when I mustered them all before the eyes of my heart, a great storm broke within me, bringing with it a great deluge of tears . . . Somehow I flung myself down beneath a fig tree and gave way to the tears which now streamed from my eyes . . . I had much to say to you, my God. . . . For I felt that I was still the captive of my sins, and in my misery I kept crying, "How long shall I go on saying, 'tomorrow, tomorrow?'" Why not now? Why not make an end of my ugly sins at this moment?

I was asking myself these questions, weeping all the while with the most bitter sorrow in my heart, when all at once I heard the singsong voice of a child in a nearby house. Whether it was the voice of a boy or a girl, I cannot say, but again and again it repeated the refrain, "Take it and read, take it and read." I stemmed my flood of tears and stood up, telling myself that this could only be a divine command to open my book of Scripture and read the first passage on which my eyes should fall. . . . I seized [the book containing Paul's Epistles] and opened it, and in silence I read the first passage on which my eyes fell: "Not in reveling and drunkenness, not in lust and wantonness, not in quarrels and rivalries . . . Rather arm yourselves with the Lord Jesus Christ . . ." I had no wish to read more and no need to do so. For in an instant, as I came to the end of the sentence, it was as though the

> light of confidence flooded into my heart and all the darkness of doubt was dispelled.
>
> I marked the place with my finger . . . and closed the book . . . You converted me to yourself.[1]

These words are from what is considered to be the first autobiography in the Western world, St. Augustine's *Confessions*, in which he recounts his conversion to Christianity. The Bible tells us that "faith comes by hearing, and hearing the Word of God," but for Augustine, faith comes by reading, reading the Word of God.

Take it and read. Reading can be a life-giving portal to another world, a whole new world. Dr. Seuss was right, "The more that you read, the more things you will know. The more that you learn, the more places you'll go."[2] You may end up in Narnia or New York right in your living room. Professors get paid to read. People read for pleasure, joining reading groups and book clubs. People read to be in community even if it is just with the author. By reading, we learn that we are not alone. A book can be a faithful, well-worn companion. There is no university without books. A common question among university types is, "What are you reading these days?" One writer notes that he's frequently asked if he were shipwrecked and could have only one book with him, what would it be? The answer he always gives is "*How to Build a Boat*." Books can be very useful friends.

These days, reading companions and habits are in transition. Kindles, Nooks, and iPads have paved the way for e-books. The nature of libraries in a digital age is changing, so that some even question the future of hardback or paperback books on shelves. But some of us still like to feel and fold the binding of a book. We like to hold it and caress it, highlight it with a yellow or pink highlighter—those favorite phrases or words or paragraphs that jarred us with joy. We like to write free associative ideas, stories, and memories in the margins to create a literary quilt of intertextuality. And don't forget about the delicious smell of old, leather-bound books. We can even touch their skin and imagine their age and their autobiography, unlike e-books that seem to never grow old and appear sterile, forever without wrinkles.

On top of that, in this digital, Internet, sound-bite, YouTube video clip society, our culture seems more attuned to a quick scanning of a text while e-surfing rather than engaging in a close reading. One takes up and reads while on the run (but hopefully not while driving). And the Bible may even be approached solely as a quick fix or quick answer for an immediate situation—to name it and claim it and then drop it to move on to the next activity, searching for one image, one

1. Augustine, *Confessions*, Book VIII.12, 177–78.
2. Seuss, *I Can Read With My Eyes Shut.*

word, one phrase, a spiritual pill to pop in my soul for the day ahead but not necessarily something to digest deeply as a revelatory door to God.

A cursory reading of this parable from Matthew may cause us to react with a wide and even loud spiritual yawn in our favorite pew or rocking chair. It's a typical story told by Jesus to push the buttons of the religious and political powers of his day. Nothing extraordinary. Nothing unexpected. On the surface, as the church has read it for centuries, this parable is an allegory. The landowner is God. The vineyard is Israel. The tenants are Jewish leaders. The servants are prophets and the son, who was thrown out of the vineyard and killed, is Jesus. Straightforward at first sight, right? But we may see and not really see. Hear and not really hear. In other words, we may not be paying attention and even miss church bulletin typos like the one that said, "The senior choir invites any member of the congregation who enjoys sinning to join the choir."

There may even be allusions in what we read, but we can miss them and by doing so we may miss a deeper meaning. English professors tell us that you can't fully understand *Moby Dick, Paradise Lost, East of Eden,* or *The Lion, the Witch, and the Wardrobe* if you don't recognize the biblical allusions in those books. If you miss the connections, the tenor of literary truth will ring more hollow. You may miss something if you rush and read, but if we slow down and possess what French philosopher and mystic Simon Weil calls the "faculty of attention" directed toward God, you may see and receive something unexpected.

It is said that Michelangelo, the great Italian sculptor, painter, and poet, who painted the ceiling of the Sistine Chapel and designed the dome of St. Peter's Basilica in Rome, once stood before a great block of marble that had been rejected by builders and cast aside. As he stood there with eyes staring straight at the marble, a friend approached and asked what he was looking at. And he said, "An angel." He saw what the mallet, the chisel, and skill could do with that rejected stone. Michelangelo said, "I saw the angel in the marble and carved until I set him free." He saw the unexpected and produced one of his masterpieces.

Michelangelo was like Sojourner Truth, who once said, "I don't read such small stuff as letters. I read men and nations."[3] Michelangelo read stones. Reading is paying attention. He saw below the surface to a deeper level. Have you ever read a stone? Stones have stories to tell, like the Petoskey stones from the lower peninsula of Michigan. They're fossilized colony corals and they can tell of their long history and what it's like to spend the day on beaches, in ditches or gravel pits, and how people study them and use them to have

3. Painter, *Sojourner Truth*, 230.

throwing contests. They can tell you about their excitement when the Michigan legislature made them the state stone. Have you ever read a stone?

On the surface when Jesus says, "The stone that the builders rejected has become the cornerstone," it may seem like no big deal. But if we're paying attention, if we read closely, that one image opens up an entire biblical universe. Stones. The Ten Commandments were written on tablets of stone (Exod 34). Joshua uses twelve stones as a memorial for the children of Israel to remember how they crossed the Jordan River on dry ground (Josh 4). David fought Goliath with five smooth stones (1 Sam 17). Samuel took a stone and called it Ebenezer (1 Sam 7). The people of God are sometimes described as having a "heart of stone" (Ezek 36). The psalmist boldly declares that "you will not dash your foot against a stone" (Ps 91). Just like in this parable, the first Christian martyr, Stephen, is stoned to death in the book of Acts. Stones can be threats and sources of danger, as when Jesus declares, "The one who falls on this stone will be broken to pieces; and it will crush anyone on whom it falls"(cf. Isa 8:14; Dan 2:34–55, 44–45).

But when you read more deeply and pay attention, you will recognize that in 1 Peter you can be built up as living stones into a spiritual temple (1 Pet 2). And these stones rest on "a tested stone, a precious cornerstone, of a sure foundation"(Isa 28) in Jesus Christ. And at the end of Jesus's life, which is where we are headed in Matthew, someone rolled a stone against the entrance of the tomb where Jesus lay (Mark 15). If we hurry, we may act like we're stoned and never read in a way that lets the stone tell the whole story of its life, and then we may risk missing the presence of Michelangelo angels. What are we missing when we don't pay attention? It's possible to see someone or something we love and still not pay attention to them or it. The way we read the world perhaps has been ruined.

Jesus's own question, "Have you never read?" is an indictment against our reading habits. It's a probing about whether we are actually paying attention to what is going on around us. This is not about whether you are a walking bibliophile or about the quantity of read books; it is about the quality of your spiritual insight and intuition. Are you paying attention? Have you never read? Reading is knowledge, power, and freedom, which is why there was resistance to teaching the enslaved in this country how to read; however, this isn't really about a literate culture over against an illiterate one, to shame the latter, because some of the wisest and most discerning people I know can't read letters but read people so well. They pay attention and know how to *really* read closely. Have you never read?

Does our reading lead to revelation about God, the world, and us? Maybe we just see stones when in fact they point to so much more. Maybe we just read about "a landowner who planted a vineyard, put a fence around it, dug a wine press in it, and built a watchtower" and think that it's a nice agricultural story for an agrarian society, but if we read closely and more deeply we may recognize that it alludes to the world of Isaiah chapter 5 with similar imagery, a world with a haunting question in the background—"when I expected it to yield grapes, why did it yield wild grapes?" If we pay attention, that Old Testament blues question is a theme right here in the New Testament vineyard.

Jesus presents an old theme with a new variation, but it still resounds with the same blues notes of unmet expectations. The landowner doesn't have his expectations met because he experiences the unexpected with the bad behavior of his tenants. He did everything by the book, yet in the biblical backdrop is the same haunting query—"when I expected it to yield grapes why did it yield wild grapes?" Have you never read? If not, you may not hear this note, but it is there in the subtext of the biblical text; though we may not see nor hear something because we're not paying attention, doesn't make it any less present or real. The landowner thinks that the tenants will respect his son but they kill him. I can't help but hear Isaiah's haunting question on his lips. The landowners who controlled the rural regions of the Roman Empire had the social and legal power to enforce rules; they even had hired assassins to deal with troublesome tenants like these, but the landowner doesn't retaliate. All of this is unexpected, even how Jesus responds.

He does respond with the common practice of expounding a Scripture by citing other Scriptures, Scripture interpreting Scripture, the Word of God using the Word of God to interpret the Word of God. "Have you never read in the scriptures: The stone that the builders rejected has become the cornerstone; this was the Lord's doing, and it is amazing in our eyes?" Of course, we've read but maybe we've only conditioned ourselves to see what is there on the surface and haven't paid attention to what is underneath.

Under these circumstances, especially if the parable is about the murdered son who is Jesus, this is a strange response from the one headed to the Golgotha gallows. He's worried about reading at a time like this and showing off his Scripture memorization from Sunday school class? Maybe he's calling us to pay attention, not only to himself as the cornerstone or capstone, but to how he responds. What he quotes is Psalm 118, a Hallel psalm, a liturgy of thanksgiving in the temple to give thanks to God for festival worship. If we read closely, what he does is lift up a form of praise as political practice and protest, because praise says, "Up to God and down to the other gods." This is unexpected from Jesus, this subtle linguistic form of the middle finger in the face of the powers that be. Praise in his mouth, a hallel-ujah, on his way to death, rejects his rejection.

Not only has Jesus been telling the disciples that the rulers would kill him (16:21; 17:23; 20:18), the Hallel psalms were sung before and after the

Passover meal (Matt 21:9; 26:30; Mark 14:26), thus his articulation of this psalm foreshadows the upcoming Passover, his death. If we never read, we may never catch the irony of the Hallel in Jesus's hell. If we never read, we may think it ludicrous for a Messiah to die. But when we approach the Bible or the communion table and pay attention, we may not only hear "take it and read," we may hear "take and eat" because the Word of God is also the bread of life. Where others see only stones, if we pay attention, we may also see angels and even Jesus.

Let me share a story I told earlier. In the aftermath of the 2010 Haiti earthquake, there was a Haitian man trapped under a slab of concrete from a collapsed building. He lay on his side as the weight of this piece of concrete rested on top of him, crushing him. All of this was caught on camera. What's crazy is that a CNN news reporter was right there, ready to get high ratings. The reporter conducted an interview with this man as he lay on his side underneath a slab of cement, and this is what she asked—"What are you telling yourself?" Well, what do you think he's telling himself as a cement block rests on top of his body, squeezing the life out of him? "I forgot to put out the garbage today or respond to that email? Or, I really would like a dirty chai latte from Starbucks?" "What are you telling yourself?!" This man should have said, "I'm asking myself why a news reporter is interviewing me right now!"

But in response to the reporter's question, "What are you telling yourself?" this man says, "Jesus, my life is in your hands." At first glance, we may just see a man dying and whose body is breaking under the weight of a building, but if we pay attention, we may see and hear Jesus under the brutal weight of the world. Have you never read, "Father, into your hands I commit my spirit"?

I don't know what happened to that man in Haiti, but I know what happened to Jesus. Yet if you never read, if you never pay attention, you may never find your redemption and know how near it is. A conversion. An angel. Jesus. Just pay attention and keep reading. You'll soon come across another stone but this one will be rolled away.

Questions about the Question

- What books have you read that have impacted you?
- What and who are you reading these days?
- What inhibits close readings?

18

What should we do?

(Luke 3:7–19)

John must be having a pretty bad day, because what kind of sermon introduction is that? "You brood of vipers!" That's no way to begin a sermon. "Fourscore and seven years ago" or "Ladies and gentlemen," maybe, but "You brood of vipers!"? He wouldn't win any seminary preaching contests with that. And I can guarantee that he wouldn't be voted in as the next bishop of the United Methodist Church either. You wouldn't ask him to join your pastoral staff. Can you imagine his pastoral care sessions? John wouldn't be your first choice to run a church growth seminar. But John is up to something else.

He's not concerned with building a spiritual fan club. He's a weirdo in the wilderness but he's got a word from the Lord. It's funny how God seems to use weirdos all the time—just look at us! John proclaims a word that slays and a word that saves. Proclaiming a baptism of repentance for the forgiveness of sins. A tough word but a truthful one. Not a happy-clappy proclamation but one that will help for sure. So just when I thought John had it all wrong homiletically, I realized that he actually had it right. He was sick and tired of being sick and tired of the same old, same old slick and sleek self-serving spirituality that was only concerned with a beautiful Sunday liturgy with its magnificent Sunday music and without any real engagement with the sick and insane and widows and poor and orphans and bullied of the world. He was tired of Jesus talk without justice walk. His sermon introduction gets the crowd's attention and it gets ours too, though

I don't recommend we pass the peace by saying "you brood of vipers!" It works for John but it might not work for us in this day and age. But he wants his listeners to know that this is serious and if they miss this, they miss the whole point of following God.

The crowds come out to be baptized. In other words, they come out to "wade in the water." But John's not interested in singing a melody that just floats into a sea of forgetfulness. He's not satisfied with singing a song and then going home to watch a college basketball game. He knows that Christian baptism, worship, is more than a song. He calls for something that will last, something that is concrete. And his message is not cheap grace. He says "Bear fruits worthy of repentance," suggesting that a repentant life will reveal itself in right living. Don't say "We have Abraham as our ancestor," as if that will let you off the hook to live a fruitless life. "We've been a part of the Methodist Church since it was founded." Don't rely on religious memory. Don't rely on the past and the good old days. Don't rely on past borne fruit that was once fresh and juicy but now is stale and rotten. Don't rely on someone else to do for you, to bear fruit that only you can bear. Don't rely on someone else's salvation, someone else's piety, someone else's baptism, what they used to do in the church and how they used to run this or that ministry. If you just rely on a past piety ("we have Abraham as our ancestor"), you may be satisfied to just go and sit down at the coffee hour after church and think that your Christian duty is done for the week. "I've embodied the baptized life, sipping my nonfat Starbucks caramel macchiato with whip," all because of "Father Abraham." This faulty reliance on the past will not do for John. Doing this, in fact, is doing nothing. Solely celebrating history may lead to perpetual inactivity. This praise of an ancient piety may lead you to only pray while others act as a sign of their baptismal repentance. To pray without prayerful action may actually get you into trouble.

You might have heard about the missionary who was walking in Africa when he heard the ominous noise of a lion behind him. "Oh Lord," prayed the missionary, "grant in Thy goodness that thc lion walking behind me is a good Christian lion." And then, in the silence that followed, the missionary heard the lion praying too: "Oh Lord, I thank Thee for the food which I am about to receive." Sometimes you can't just pray. You need to do something like run away or at least run while praying. I'm not knocking prayer. But I am saying that praying without prayerfully acting is the source of an anorexic faith. There is an integral relationship between contemplation and action. We see a great example of this in the ministry of Dr. King, as spelled out in Vanderbilt historian Lewis Baldwin's book *Never to Leave Us Alone*. Doing nothing in the Christian life will make you spiritually thin and eventually lead to death. You may not be eaten by a lion but you will get burned.

And John confirms this. Bearing no good fruit, doing nothing that helps someone else, leads to a spiritual death. "The axe is lying at the root of the trees" and trees that bear bad fruit will be cut down and thrown into the fire, burned up because no good fruit is borne from their life. Burned up because we are too comfortable sitting on the Methodist hymnal in a cushy pew. Devoured by a lion because of inactivity. Burned up because we are more interested in the glory days of Methodist religiosity than the present days of Methodist renewal and reformation. And because of this fire of judgment that rains down on a do-nothing Christianity, the chant "burn baby burn" takes on new meaning. But this does not mean that people are not doing anything. Maybe they are doing the wrong thing, bearing bad fruit.

The type of fruit that causes people to play god with guns by shooting up fellow human beings whenever they want. The type of fruit that says you are pro-life except when it comes to the death penalty. The type of fruit that bullies folk just because they're different. The type of fruit that equates being Christian with being an American. The type of fruit that burns other religions' sacred texts in the name of Jesus, causing Christianity to be equated with hatred and not the healing balm of Gilead. The type of fruit that hides behind a hypocritical Christianity that does and says one thing in the pulpit and another thing in everyday life.

This is what not to do and so the crowds, seeing what some Christians tend to do, ask John, "What should we do?" Crowds and "the world" usually get a bad rap in our day, so you hear, "don't follow the crowd." But in this story, the crowd's peer pressure would actually lead to authentic faithful living. The crowd gets it. They want to do Christian, not just be Christian, as a counter-narrative to the kind of discipleship that makes some people say atheists make better Christians than Christians themselves, because they actually will do something. The crowd reveals that baptismal discipleship costs something, does something. It requires something from us. Repentance then forgiveness of sins. It is costly, thus the crowd asks the right question. "What should we do?" It happens three times to get our attention like a repetitive righteous rap—what should we do, what should we do, what should we do. And the answers they receive are very practical, down-to-earth responses, theology in the flesh, in the world, on the backs, in the mouths, in the pockets of real people, not behind the corridors of denominational headquarters in a committee meeting where we talked about the last committee meeting where we talked about the last committee meeting.

What should we do? "Whoever has two coats must share with anyone who has none; and whoever has food must do likewise." What should we do? "Collect no more than the amount prescribed for you." What should we do? "Do not extort money from anyone by threats or false accusation, and be satisfied with your wages." Selfless sharing, anti-economic bullying, being content with what one has. Basically, "don't be greedy," thinking more is ministry, like the prosperity gospel gurus. Actually, selfless sharing may signify your own satisfaction with what God has already given you.

And what I love about this passage is that baptism is linked to mission in the world. Baptism has everything to do with social and economic justice. Baptism is not just a little sprinkling of water or full immersion in a pool, baptism is being plunged into a new way of living, being, and acting in the world. Baptism immerses you into the ethics of Jesus and is connected to social responsibility and service towards others. Your conversion to Christianity, signified in your baptism, converts, literally turns you towards God, and your turn to God is also a turn to the other. The invisible grace of the sacrament of baptism becomes visible in outward mission. Our baptism is not just for us but for others. We're baptized to be a blessing to someone else. Our baptism is interlocked with an ethic of generosity. Methodist liturgical historian James White says it best: "We undertake in baptism a serious responsibility not only for the spiritual welfare but also the material welfare of our fellow members of the body of Christ. The two cannot be separated. The deprivation of our neighbor is a sign of our failure to take our baptism seriously. On the other hand, deeds of love and charity are a form of living out our baptism."[1] Not an either/or but a both/and. Not just a baptismal rite but right action. Not just a sacrament but also service. Not just heavenly minded, but earthly good. Not just spiritually ignited, but socially engaged. Not just personal piety but social witness. Not just works of piety but works of mercy. Not just the liturgy but the liturgy after the liturgy. Not just the water of the Spirit but the work of the Spirit. Not just lip service but life service. Christian rhetoric and a Christian ethic.

"What should we do?" is a call for Christian liturgical integrity. This is why one poet writes that he'd rather see a sermon than hear one any day. St. Augustine argues that your life can be an eloquent sermon.[2] "What should we do?" says that we should do something. It reminds me of the words of Dr. Martin Luther King Jr., in his sermon "The Three Dimensions of a Complete Life." In it, he says, "What did you do for others?"[3] What are you doing for others? What are you doing for others even if you get nothing in return?

> A young man shopping in a supermarket noticed an elderly woman following him around. If he stopped, she stopped and she kept staring at him. She finally overtook him at the checkout

1. White, *Sacraments in Protestant Practice and Faith*, 71.
2. See Augustine, *On Christian Teaching*, Book IV.
3. King, "Three Dimensions of a Complete Life."

> counter, turned to him and said, "I hope I haven't made you feel ill at ease; it's just that you look so much like my late son." He answered, "That's okay." And she said, "I know it's silly, but if you'd call out 'Goodbye, Mom' as I leave the store, it would make me feel so happy." She then went through the checkout, and as she was on her way out of the store, the man called out, "Goodbye, Mom." The elderly woman waved and smiled back at him. He was so pleased that he had brought a little sunshine into someone's day. He then went to pay for his groceries. "That comes to $121.85," said the clerk. The man was stunned, "How come so much? I only bought 5 items!" The clerk replied, "Yeah, but your mother said you'd be paying for her things, too."[4]

What are you doing for others even if you get nothing in return? You act, not for reciprocity, but because you are redeemed. You are washed and it should make a difference. What should we do in light of our baptism?

With all of this emphasis on what we should do, I should caution that we aren't in charge or calling the shots because it's not really our mission; it's God's. But when we want to take charge and we act for our own wishes, things may get off track and there might be a downfall, literally. At my college graduation many years ago, Mae Jemison told a story about a cowboy and a horse named Speedy. A cowboy was trying to find a fast horse. He needed to find the fastest horse he could because he needed to get from the East Coast to the West Coast immediately. So he went all over town, trying to find this horse. He finally heard about this horse named Speedy. He went directly to the farmer and said, "I understand you have the fastest horse in town." The farmer said, "Yup, that's right. Not only that, he's the fastest horse on the East Coast." The cowboy said, "I don't need to hear any more. Just give him to me. Let me give you some money." The farmer said, "Hold on. I can't sell you Speedy until I give you some instructions first." The cowboy said, "I don't need any instructions. I've been riding horses all my life." The farmer said, "Well, I can't sell you Speedy 'til I give you some instructions." The cowboy said, "All right. What are they?" The farmer said, "Speedy will not go 'til you say, 'Praise the Lord.'" The cowboy said "fine," and started counting out the money. The farmer said, "Hold on. I have some more instructions." The cowboy said, "What are they?" The farmer said, "Speedy will not stop unless you say 'Amen.'" The cowboy said, "All right. Are there any more instructions?" The farmer said, "No, that's it."

So the cowboy counted out the money, jumped on Speedy and said, "Giddy up. Let's go." Speedy didn't go anywhere. The cowboy kicked Speedy

4. "Goodbye Mum."

in the side. "Giddy up." Speedy just sat there. Finally, the cowboy remembered. He said, "Praise the Lord," and Speedy shot out like a bullet. Speedy was *boogedy, boogedy, boogedy*. Speedy was going so fast, he ran over the Appalachian Mountains and the cowboy's ears popped. *Boogedy, boogedy, boogedy*. He tore up the Indiana cornfields, jumped over the Mississippi River, through the St. Louis Arch. Speedy was gone, *boogedy, boogedy, boogedy*. Jumped over the Grand Canyon and tore up the Great Salt Lake—not necessarily in that order. Came up and over the Sierra Nevada Mountains, looked at Lake Tahoe. The cowboy looked out and saw the Pacific Ocean shining clearly, and Speedy was still going *boogedy, boogedy, boogedy*. They came up to a cliff. But Speedy was not stopping. The cowboy started getting nervous. He started saying, "Whoa, Speedy, slow down." Speedy was still going *boogedy, boogedy, boogedy*. They were almost at the cliff, and the cowboy was pulling on the reins, but Speedy wouldn't stop. They were at the cliff, and the cowboy remembered. He said, "Amen." Speedy stopped on a dime. Right at the edge of the cliff, with hooves barely holding on. The cowboy was really happy because he had made it from the East Coast to the West Coast in two hours. He was so happy, in fact, that he reared back, grinning from ear to ear, and said, "Praise the Lord!" If it's only about what we do and what we want, we are in trouble and cliffs are in our future!

But John just doesn't leave us with what we should do but leaves us with what God has done in Jesus Christ. "I baptize you with water; but one who is more powerful than I is coming . . . He will baptize you with the Holy Spirit and fire." Your generosity is important and "what should we do?" is a vital question, but be careful not to praise justice more than Jesus and focus only on human agency at the expense of Christology. John helps us to see our generosity in light of God's generosity. "What should we do?" should remind us of what God has already done in Christ and what God is doing. That "One who is more powerful than I is coming" and has come. John has a powerful ministry but watch out for Jesus! He's so powerful that he demonstrated strength in weakness as he became poor and hungry and naked. So much power that he was baptized unto death to serve us life. Jesus met and meets our needs when we don't expect it or deserve it. He looked beyond our faults and saw our need. God saw that we needed clothes and became clothed in our skin. God saw that we needed food and became daily bread for us. God saw that we were thirsty and poured life-giving blood in us. Christ's life is cruciform love and this love is like the Energizer bunny—it keeps going and going and going and going. Going against all the odds. Going against the latest political polls. Going for those in need.

In the classic TV series *M*A*S*H*, set in a mobile army hospital during the Korean War, doctors received a patient who believed he was Jesus

Christ. Arnold Chandler had been a bombardier and had dropped many bombs on other human beings. Because of the trauma of it all, one day his mind snapped and he decided that he was no longer a man named Arnold Chandler. He was Christ the Lord. This appeared to be a mental condition that would require a lot of therapy. A psychiatrist eventually came to the man and said, "You say you are Christ, and yet here you are in an army hospital in the middle of a war. What would Jesus be doing here?" With tears streaming down his face, this supposedly mentally ill man replied with these words: "I am Christ the Lord, where else should I be? These are my children."[5]

Jesus goes to the places of pain and goes all the way to the cross. He risked it all for the world, even unto death, because baptism kills you for the life of the world—for the rich and poor, male/female, young/old, black/white, Latino/Asian, straight/gay, Democrat/Republican, West Coast Methodist/East Coast Methodist, Duke Divinity and even Harvard Divinity. Because Jesus has done so much for us, we can't help but do for others—that is a sign of being baptized in the Spirit. What we should do is discovered through what Jesus has done and is doing.

Not everyone will like what is done. Not every will agree with what is done. John was thrown in prison. Jesus was thrown on a cross. But we know he kept on doing and his doing keeps us going today. "What should we do?" Remember your baptism. You died to live and because you died someone else should live. A life worth living is affirming the worth of every life.

If I can help somebody
As I travel along
If I can help somebody with a word or song
If I can help somebody from doing wrong
My living shall not be in vain.[6]

Questions about the Question

- What do you feel called to do in this moment?
- How do you live out your baptism?
- Would John's message resonate with today's world?

5. As described in Hoezee, *Actuality*, 113.
6. Androzzo, "If I Can Help Somebody."

19

Why do you stand looking up toward heaven?

(Acts 1:6–11)

Why are you standing here? It's a question raised out of the sacred pages of these Scriptures. It's a question two men in white robes ask the disciples, "Why do you stand looking up toward heaven?" We may approach the Bible when we read it as if we are righteous lawyers interrogating the holy writ, as if we are the only ones asking questions, putting it on trial. But what we will discover is that we aren't the only ones asking questions. We are being questioned, not by two men in white robes and not even by the Bible, but by a living God. There's a question we have to answer—why are you standing here?

There are other questions in the Bible that we hear repeated and discussed more often than the one posed today. Jesus asks on the cross, "My God, my God why have you forsaken me?" Jesus asks Peter, "Who do you say that I am?" Mary asks, when she learns that she will give birth to Jesus, "How can this be since I am virgin?" Pilate asks Jesus, "What is truth?" The lamenting psalmist raises his own question, "How long, O Lord?" Questioning is a part of the life of faith. The previous questions we may have heard before and perhaps they make the top ten list of questions in the Bible. Yet there are other questions that may not make Jerusalem headline news and are tucked away in the obituary section in the back of the newspaper. These questions are not dead, but we may not want to face their tough interrogation. Yet, they are still relevant for living today and one in particular screams to be answered: "Why are you standing here?"

That's not the only question posed in this pericope. The disciples ask Jesus, "Lord, is this the time when you will restore the kingdom to Israel?" Some questions have no human answers. The disciples want to know, "What are you going to do Jesus?" But they'll soon learn that's not any of their concern. And Jesus does just like Jesus does—keeps them off balance and says, "It is not for you to know the times or periods that the Father has set by his own authority." "It is not for you to know." We want to be in the know so badly, but if we knew everything there is to know we wouldn't have to trust anymore. We would need no faith if we knew it all. If we knew it all, we probably couldn't handle it all. If we knew it all, we would be God. And as I survey the universal church, I'm glad none of us are god.

Our calling as disciples is not to know everything there is to know. It's okay to ask questions with the recognition that Jesus is not obligated to answer. "It's not for you to know." There's no insider information for disciples. You may ask someone whom you encounter in daily life, "How are you doing today?" and if they respond with "I'm well, as far as I know," they speak the truth. "As far as I know" indicates that our knowledge can only go so far because there are finite limits on what we know and every now and then we need to be reminded that "it is not for us to know." And even though we don't know, we can still be disciples because knowledge is not a prerequisite for discipleship. Systematic theology in formal theological education in seminaries may attempt to systematize God but the irony is that God cannot be controlled or locked into any human system. We can't know everything God does. "The wind blows where it wills, and you hear the sound of it, but you don't know from where it comes or where it goes" (John 3:8).

There are some things that we can't know or will never know. On May 1, 1915, the *Lusitania*, the British transatlantic passenger liner ship, considered the "greyhound of the seas," left New York for its 202nd crossing. At the time there were tensions between Britain and Germany, while the United States remained officially neutral.

While eleven miles off the coast of Ireland on May 7, 1915, people aboard the ship heard and felt a sharp explosion. A torpedo from a German submarine had struck the right side toward the bow. Seconds later, a massive internal explosion rocked the ship and it immediately started sinking. The *Lusitania* disappeared beneath the waves in eighteen minutes. Some 1,198 men, women, and children—among them 128 Americans—perished. The *Lusitania*'s destruction set off a diplomatic battle between Britain, Germany, and the United States. The 128 American casualties were enough for some to advocate for armed retaliation and America ultimately declared war against Germany in 1917.

Meanwhile, there was lots of speculation about the sinking. What caused the second, fatal explosion—a boiler's coal or gunpowder? There were conspiracy theories. The German embassy accused Britain of smuggling military weapons aboard the liner, which the British denied. Others claimed that Britain conspired to have the ship destroyed as a way to force American entry into the war. Why did the ship sink so fast, and was there a cover-up? These are lingering mysteries.

We may hunt for answers but still only questions will remain. Who was behind the assassinations of John F. Kennedy or Martin Luther King Jr.? Why did Amelia Earhart and her plane disappear as she flew over the Pacific Ocean in 1937? Why is it that when you transport something by car, it is called a shipment, but when you transport something by ship, it is called cargo? Questions, which some say will never be truly answered. We really have to un-know the idea that we should know everything. People still waste their spiritual energy on predicting the end times when we've been told it will happen like a thief in the night and no one knows the hour. Yet we continue to desire insider information while it is not for us to always know. According to philosopher Socrates, "The only true wisdom is in knowing you know nothing."

This may be disheartening because we believe the idea that "knowledge is power." The more knowledge we have, we assume the more power we will have as well. The more intellectual ascension the more strength we possess. Brighter means stronger within this frame of thought. But this concept falls off the ethical cliff when we think we are better than others because we have more knowledge—the stronger ones are the smarter ones, which then creates a hierarchy of humanity, putting the literati at the top and the least of these at the bottom. Toni Morrison implicitly warns against this when she reminisces about reading to her grandmother. She says, "I have suspected, more often than not, that I know more than she did, that I know more than my grandfather and my great-grandmother did, but I also know that I'm no wiser than they were. And whenever I have tried earnestly to diminish their vision and prove to myself that I know more, and when I have tried to speculate on their interior life and match it up with my own, I have been overwhelmed every time by the richness of theirs compared to my own."[1] As the apostle Paul noted, "knowledge puffs up" (1 Cor 8:1). The gospel suggests that knowledge doesn't even lead to power. Knowledge is impotent in the light of the power of God.

1. Morrison, "Site of Memory," 356.

In fact, it seems as if the power may come from not knowing. "It is not for you to know . . . But you will receive power when the Holy Spirit has come upon you" (Acts 1:8). We don't have to know in order to receive a gift from God. Not knowing doesn't preclude you from having power and knowledge is not a qualification for being a disciple of Jesus.

Knowledge is not a requirement for being a witness to Christ; rather, power is the power of the Holy Spirit. Power. *Dunamis*, from which we get the word "dynamite." This power is explosive and expansive, so why in the world are you just standing looking up toward heaven? Why are you standing here, if you've received dynamite power? Your life should have an explosive influence in the world.

The power of the Holy Spirit is not for heaven. The power of God is for work on earth—"you will be my witnesses . . ." We don't need witnesses in heaven. We need them on earth. The Holy Spirit is not an escape hatch to heaven. The Spirit empowers you for ministry on earth. Disciples are not supposed to be "gazing up" (1:10), so heavenly-minded that they neglect doing earthly good. The disciples are called back to earth, "to the ends of the earth" (1:8). Why are you standing looking up? The power of the Spirit baptizes you in the world, not apart from it. Jesus's ascension is not about our ascent but about our descent into deeper mission on earth due to the descent of the Spirit. Jesus is lifted up that the power of the Spirit might be let loose in our lives.

So why are you standing here when your life is a temple of the dynamite of God? Why are you standing here, looking away from earth to avoid real, everyday issues? Why are you standing here? Has the dynamite dimmed or been destroyed? Is the fire shut up in your bones gone? Why do you stand looking up to heaven when there is so much work to do in the church and world?

A Pew Research Center study called "America's Changing Religious Landscape,"[2] based on a survey of 35,000 American adults, shows the Christian percentage of the US population dropping to 70.6 percent. In 2007, the last time Pew conducted a similar survey, 78.4 percent of American adults called themselves Christian. Also, almost every major branch of Christianity in the United States has lost a significant number of members, mainly because millennials (those born between 1980 and 1999) are leaving the church. More than one-third of millennials say they are unaffiliated with any faith, which is up 10 percentage points since 2007. People who profess no faith affiliation—often called the "nones"—are now nearly 23 percent of the country's adult population, putting the unaffiliated nearly

2. See "America's Changing Religious Landscape."

on par with evangelicals (25.4 percent) and ahead of Catholics (about 21 percent) and mainline Protestants (14.7 percent).

The long view of the generational spans is striking as well. Whereas 85 percent of the silent generation (born 1928–1945) call themselves Christians, just 56 percent of today's younger millennials (born 1990–1996) do the same, even though the vast majority—about eight in ten—were raised in religious homes. Each successive generation of Americans includes fewer Christians and a critical part of this is that older generations of Americans are not passing along the Christian faith as effectively as others did in the past. How can we stand still when this is the state of the church?

Why are you just standing here when we continue to watch young and poor and black males, in particular, get trapped in cycles of gun violence, even implicating the police at times? Why are you just standing here when thousands of people, across the world, continue to engage in public, nonviolent demonstrations as rituals of public mourning and protest? Why are you standing here when we see so much "civic estrangement"?[3]

The power, the *dunamis*, the dynamite of the Spirit, is not given because we have all the answers to society's issues; it is given and promised to break us out of our silent spiritual stagnancy. A sedentary spiritual life will kill you. The power of God is not given in order to stand still and watch from safe ecclesial sidelines. The power comes down in order to lift others up that they, too, may ascend while on earth. The disciples gather but through the Spirit's power, scatter.

Dynamite explodes and disperses illuminating fire. This power is centrifugal, moving outward, beyond what is familiar, beyond Jerusalem, the center, to "all Judea and Samaria [the margins], and to the ends of the earth." The Spirit stretches us beyond our comfort zones, our knowledge, to encounter difference and experience God in a new place and in a new way. To do this kind of boundary-crossing work, you need power. You don't need power to stay home or get stuck in a rut. You need power when you are nudged toward a transgeographical, transcultural, transethnic, translinguistic, transdisciplinary ministry, because it is more complex and beautiful when you enter unchartered territory guided by the presence of God.

We reveal that we are empowered by the Holy Spirit when we cross boundaries because the Spirit always takes us beyond ourselves, beyond what we know to the unknown, beyond our world to the entire world, out of a silo of sameness, in order to expand our hearts and minds. The power of God is not needed if we are only with those like us; we need power to deal with difference as the gospel nudges us away from denominational

3. Tillet, *Sites of Slavery*, 3.

narcissism to untraveled spiritual terrain. We need power to get our feet to pray and to risk moving beyond the normative center.

The power of God explodes our illusions in thinking what we know is the best thing to know or the only thing that can be known. The Spirit will blow up our confining theologies in order to be at "full stretch,"[4] as wide as the mercy of God for the world. Without the Spirit, our lives won't be dynamite but dead. But with the power of the Spirit, we will sense a new way, a new life, a new beginning, a new mission in the world, as we are propelled outward away from our norms toward the margins, which are made central to the gospel mission of Jesus through the power of the Spirit.

The church is to be on the move, never stagnant, always empowered by the Holy Spirit for the missional life of God in the world. God has called us to the ends of the earth to wherever and whatever is foreign or strange to us. And the power we will receive is the power to be witnesses. The question is not "Lord, are you going to do x, y, and z?" The question is, "What am I going to do? And, why am I just standing here?"

We receive power to do something, to be witnesses. French philosopher Paul Ricoeur makes four claims about being a witness. He says 1) the witness is not a volunteer but is one who is sent to testify; 2) the testimony of the witness is about God—Jesus is witnessed to in the testimony; 3) the purpose of the testimony is a proclamation to all people; 4) the testimony of the witness consists of the entire life, speech and action, of the witness.[5]

It's understandable why there may be a preference to be in the know, because to receive the power of the Spirit leads you to a place of unknowing and it is risky because to be a witness is risky. The New Testament word for witness is "martyr." The power of the Spirit received by disciples is the power to die. To be a witness for the Lord requires explosive, enduring power. Without power, there will be a weak witness. But with it, testifying can be terrifying because we know where it might lead. Dynamite can be scary or intimidating. It can explode some things that we like or hold on to. It can kill us, and we don't want to die to what we've known or what we've become used to, the way it's always been. But to witness for the Lord is a death to self and the only way that is possible is with the power of the Spirit. The power of God will cause you to put your life on the line and you can't do that standing still, gazing upward at a church bell tower.

The Spirit is calling us to receive power to be witnesses in the world, so why are you standing here? There's a whole world out there that needs

4. This is a term of liturgical theologian Don Saliers. See Anderson and Morill, eds., *Liturgy and the Moral Self.*

5. Ricoeur, "Hermeneutics of Testimony."

the love and life of Jesus. The Spirit is calling us to light up the world with spiritual dynamite. Let's do it together. There's a Spiritual called "Witness for My Lord." It begins with "My soul is a witness for the Lord" and then subsequent stanzas mention different biblical characters and the singer calls the roll—Methuselah was a witness for my Lord, Samson was a witness for my Lord, Daniel was a witness for my Lord. We know about their witness but what about yours?

A man was surprised to learn that a former professor of his, who was an atheist during his undergraduate years and once called Christianity a "helpless hangover," had become a Christian years later. He went to the professor's home and asked about his conversion. His former professor said that the pastor got to him. This former student was puzzled because he knew that his former professor could think rings around this particular pastor. But the former professor responded and said that the pastor did not outthink him, he outlived him. He was a witness.

The Spiritual ends with, "Who will be a witness for my Lord?" Will you?

Questions about the Question

- What hinders your witness and why is it easy to only stand and gaze upward?
- What are signs of God's *dunamis* in the world?
- How are you a witness for the Lord today?

20

What does this mean?
(Acts 2:1–21)

After hearing the sound of a rushing violent wind and seeing the divided tongues like fire resting on each of them and hearing those filled with the Spirit speak in other languages, it's no surprise that those present ask each other the question, "What does this mean?" Of course, some think the Christians are drunk from wine served at a college frat party. Peter assures them later that they aren't drunk at all with spirits but filled with another Spirit. "What does this mean?" It's a great question. People have been interpreting this passage for centuries, trying to figure out what the day of Pentecost means.

This Acts passage has a special place in my historical memory since I spent my childhood and adolescent years in a classical Pentecostal church. In classical Pentecostal doctrine, Acts chapter 2 is used as a prooftext to teach that the initial physical evidence of a person having received the baptism of the Holy Spirit is speaking in tongues. This experience is subsequent to conversion. I heard this doctrine my entire life. I heard and saw many things in that Miami, Florida congregation. I heard people speaking in tongues. I saw people get slain in the Spirit. I heard ecstatic music with drums, organs, guitars, and brass instruments. I saw people clapping, dancing, and shouting. I can confirm writer James Baldwin's description of his father's Pentecostal church, when he says, "I have never seen anything to equal the fire and excitement that sometimes, without warning, fill a church, causing the church, . . . to 'rock.'"[1] There weren't necessarily holy rollers but we definitely had some holy rockers.

Pentecostalism, in all its forms, has exploded all over the world and is a major force in global Christianity, such that we have charismatic Catholics, charismatic Anglicans, and more. The world's Christian population has shifted from the "North" to the global South and this shift has been due to the tremendous growth of Pentecostal communities worldwide—in sub-Saharan Africa, Latin America, and numerous parts of Asia.

As a PK, a preacher's kid, I've seen and experienced all kinds of things in the ecumenical church in general and in the church of my youth in particular. The rhythmic clapping and dancing were captivating at times, but they weren't the only things that captivated me at a young age in that congregation, because I met a little seven-year-old girl who is now my wife. Pentecost has its benefits! But what does it really mean? Or, more accurately, what are its meanings?

Liturgically, Christians celebrate Pentecost as an end of the Easter season at fifty days, linking the resurrection and ascension of Christ with the sending of the Holy Spirit. Historically, Pentecost was related to the Jewish harvest festival of Shavuot or Feast of Weeks. It commemorated the giving of the Law at Sinai but also celebrated harvesting of wheat. During this festival, people could bring their firstfruits to the temple as an offering. Using this historical lens, one might then say that Pentecost is the human experience of the firstfruits of the Spirit. The liturgical or historical significance of Pentecost is not unimportant because it is part of its meanings. What else does Pentecost mean? As Christians, it's vital to attempt to answer that question because Pentecost and Pentecostalism are not going away; it's on the rise, even if not in actual experience, but in the collective consciousness of the global church.

In the third wave of the National Congregations Study, led by Duke professor Mark Chaves, we learn that from 1998 to 2012, drumming, jumping, shouting, dancing, raising hands in praise, using visual projection, and speaking in tongues have increased in congregations, while singing by a choir and use of a written program have decreased. Worship has become more informal and ethnic diversity in congregations is on the rise.[2]

The present state of the changing church would have been more welcoming to B. B. King, the King of the Blues. In his early days, there was tension between blues music and the church. Some viewed the blues as the devil's music and believed it had no place in the church. The church was a

1. Baldwin, *Fire Next Time*, 50.

2. For further insight into this study, see NORC, "National Congregations Study."

religious gatekeeper of who's in and who's out. But what Pentecost reveals is that that which is different or foreign may actually be the gift we need. Pentecost has many meanings, but at the core of its meanings is the idea of gift.

Pentecost suggests that the ground of our spiritual life is fundamentally a divine gift. "And suddenly from heaven there *came* a sound" (2:2). The sound came. The Spirit came on divine volition. The Spirit is God's gift to us; and one of the gifts of the Spirit is the gift of multilingual speech. "All of them were filled with the Holy Spirit and began to speak in other languages, as the Spirit gave them ability" (2:4).

Some were amazed, for sure. "But others sneered and said, 'They are filled with new wine'"(2:13). People don't always understand what God is doing or what is being said or played. It's like an unknown tongue. The blues wasn't accepted in every church because it was different, but it was the blues that seemed to call B. B. King and others, even though some didn't understand the music and the man.

In 1999, in a public conversation with William Ferris, chairman of the National Endowment for the Humanities, B. B. King recounted how he came to sing the blues.

> Growing up on the plantation there in Mississippi, I would work Monday through Saturday noon. I'd go to town on Saturday afternoons, sit on the street corner, and I'd sing and play. I'd have me a hat or box or something in front of me. People that would request a gospel song would always be very polite to me, and they'd say: "Son, you're mighty good. Keep it up. You're going to be great one day." But they never put anything in the hat. But people that would ask me to sing a blues song would always tip me and maybe give me a beer. They always would do something of that kind. Sometimes I'd make 50 or 60 dollars one Saturday afternoon. Now you know why I'm a blues singer.[3]

B. B. King and the church in particular saw themselves as incommensurable with each other; there wasn't mutual understanding, but the gift of the Spirit works toward comprehension and common ground.

Another prominent gift at Pentecost is the gift of understanding. The gift of speech makes breaking news but the gift of speech is not given in order *not* to be understood. Pentecost reveals a gift of the Spirit to be hearing in one's own language. When disciples are filled with the Spirit and speak in other languages as the Spirit enables them to do so, "Jews from every nation under heaven" become bewildered and amazed because "each one heard them speaking in the native language of each" (2:5–6). "And how is it that

3. National Endowment for the Humanities, "Conversation with B. B. King."

we hear, each of us, in our own native language?"(2:8) The miracle is not the physical ability of hearing but it is the understanding of what is said, despite the different cultures of the speakers. The lens of Pentecost urges us to seek understanding, not mere hearing, and to do so across native cultures.

The Spirit engages in the work of translation by translating the Word of God into each native language present so that others may learn about God. Thus, the Word is not monolingual. Pentecost reveals the Spirit's embrace of cultural particularity and context and promotes "essentially worldwide proclamation."[4] Translation into each language demonstrates a divine care for diverse cultures, ethnicities, and languages. In the Spirit, diversity is not a dirty word but a beautiful one in the light of God. If one has problems with diversity, one has to take it up with the Spirit who creates diversity in the first place, as the gospel is expressed in particular contexts, cultures, languages, and bodies.

The range of human differences matters in the world. Through the theological lens of Acts 2, we might call "diversity" a "Pentecostal ecology." And in this ecology, the notion of gift prioritizes the work of God, yet God doesn't deny or erase human identity. Pentecost reveals that human speakers and hearers are needed for "God's deeds of power" to be known. The Spirit embraces the cultures of humanity and Pentecost suggests the flourishing of humankind, not its destruction or eradication.

To have everyone speaking English in the same manner or certain ethnic names changed to English may be questioned in the burning light of Pentecost, because Pentecost reveals that we need Parthians, Medes, Elamites, and residents of Mesopotamia, Judea and Cappadocia, Pontus and Asia, Phrygia and Pamphylia, Egypt and the parts of Libya belonging to Cyrene, and visitors from Rome, both Jews and proselytes, Cretans and Arabs. We shouldn't erase our names, our languages, our cultures, our skin color, our hair texture, the color of our eyes, the shape of our bodies, our identities. We shouldn't obliterate whom and what God has created in order to suit our needs and comforts and opinions—God made all of us with our own native tongue and when we are tempted to erase that which is different it is an affront to God and God's collective body.

Pentecost is the creation of a particular kind of human community, a God-centered community, another key gift of the Spirit. The cultural particularity of the Spirit's gift is not contrary to a universal quality. The gifts of speech and understanding reveal the common message of the Spirit: God. What the people heard in their native languages was the message about "God's deeds of power" (2:11).

4. Welker, *God the Spirit*, 230.

In whatever language, God is central, both object and subject of life in the Spirit. Pentecost privileges God as the universal content of our message through particular cultural means. The end is always God but the means is always particular, holding together the creative relationship between particularity and universality. Dietrich Bonhoeffer once preached that people were bored with the church and the cinema appeared to be more interesting than the church "because we talk too much about false, trivial human things and ideas in the church and too little about God."[5]

The Spirit will not allow us to forget about God because, "Through the pouring out of the Spirit, God effects a world-encompassing, multilingual, polyindividual testimony to Godself."[6] Though there is a diverse community, there is unity around the presence of God. It is a distinct community in which God is the center. Cultural specificity is important but in the Spirit it is decentered. God dethrones cultural or ethnic hegemony at Pentecost. But it's also necessary to note that cultural identities are not demolished either. Cultural identities are fully present and fully inspirited while the Spirit leads the people to speak about and praise God.

We can take the Spirit seriously and not hide behind or promote God as a way to homogenize the community into one totalizing paradigm. There is no homogenous universal church. Though God-centered, Pentecost reveals the gift of a community that represents boundary-breaking, bridge-making realities across culture, ethnicity, race, and language. In the Spirit there's no room for segregated enclaves. The Spirit breaks us out of our totalizing patterns, breaks us out of seeing and understanding God in only one way, one theology, one perspective. The Spirit leads us to different views and voices, a different way of seeing the world and God. The Spirit leads us to embrace diversity as a gift of God while the Spirit moves us toward integration, collaboration, and mutuality between different voices as a way to form community.

The formation of a global community through the in-breaking of the Spirit breaks humanity out of our proclivity toward sameness and moves us to embrace a broad, inclusive gospel for "the ends of the earth"(1:8). The Spirit breaks open our hearts to include all people, and as my Baptist brothers and sisters might say, to "open the doors of the church," and break us out of our tendencies to be with those who are just like us in every way. The gift of God opens us up to a hospitable vision in which the Spirit is poured out on "all flesh" (2:17), thus no one is exempt from the blessing of the Spirit being poured out over their life, regardless of race, age, gender, or class. Any

5. Bonhoeffer, "Ambassadors for Christ," 91.

6. Welker, *God the Spirit,* 235.

person anywhere can be a conduit of the Spirit. There's no limit to whom or where the gospel can be preached because the gospel travels and knows no bounds as the Spirit creates a diverse human community. Pentecost suggests that the Spirit opens us up to the possibility of hospitable relationships across cultures as opposed to closed off systems that restrict the full scope of the gospel of God. This means Bach and Brahms can be in the same spiritual family as B. B. King and Branford Marsalis. Hymns and hip hop may actually commune with each other when the Spirit blows.

The promise of Pentecost is that even though we may not speak the same language, we serve the same God and are members of the same community built on the love of Christ. Without different tongues or languages, the fire of the Spirit might be dimmer, but with one another from every tribe and nation in the unity of the Spirit, we may come to understand the light and beauty of God in a fuller way. The gift of this community is that it is "not a homogenous unity, but a differentiated one."[7] Pentecost represents the preservation and goodness of human diversity in God's community. The church is called to be unified, not uniform. We aren't the church when we are uniform; we are the church in the power of the Spirit when we are unified, a unified diversity focused on God. And this is a powerful witness in a world that is so divided. Pentecost reminds us of the unmerited gift of God resting on all flesh like fire that doesn't destroy but builds, creates, and invites us to a deeper communion.

From the cosmopolitan church of my youth, I remember Brother Hing, Brother Keith, Brother Timms, Brother Mack. I remember Sister Timms, Sister Santiche, Sister Bostwick. I remember the cloud of witnesses, including Sister Jean. She had a big smile on her face and a bounce in her step every Sunday. We sang in the choir together when I was a teenager. I can still hear her greeting me—"Hi, Brother Luke." She had a way of saying it—"Brother Luke." After several years passed after high school, I went back home to Miami expecting to hear good news about the sweet elder Christian sisters from my youth. Instead, I found out that the bounce in Sister Jean's step had been stolen. Stolen by a sickness that was decaying her body. She still went to church. She even had special seating. A couch was placed right in the front of the sanctuary near the pulpit platform. They put it there so she could still hear the hymns of faith. They put it there so she could rest when needed. Her heart still sang even though it was broken. Broken because the disease she had was AIDS, contracted from her very own husband who had been fooling around. A God-fearing, churchgoing woman with AIDS.

7. Welker, *God the Spirit,* 228.

Pentecost reveals that the church is not made in our image but in the mosaic image of God. It shows us that the beauty of God is more fully revealed in the collective face of others and the beauty of God is distorted when particular cultures and languages are muted because they are different. The image of God at Pentecost is multilingual, multicultural, and multiethnic, not for a politically correct agenda, but because the gospel demands it. The gospel and the church are polyphonic.

In other words, your voice matters. Be yourself, not an imitation of someone else. *You* are a gift—old, young, male, female, PhD or no D at all, professor or student, northerner or southerner, healthy or sick, whether you sit in a pew, an auditorium chair, or a couch. There are gifts of the Spirit and Pentecost reveals that you are a gift of the Spirit, with your particular culture, ethnicity, voice, language, body, idiosyncrasies, interests, fields, and talents; some of you with hair, and others of you without so much hair. You have something to contribute to the church and world that only you can do. Emory professor Gregory Ellison told me a long time ago, "Do you." What does Pentecost mean? If you don't do you, we can't really do us.

Questions about the Question

- What is the relationship between diversity and unity?
- What does Pentecost mean to you?
- How does the Holy Spirit work in your life, at work, and in your churches?

21

Where have they come from?

(Rev 7:9–17)

We often pray the Lord's Prayer and make the plea "on earth as it is in heaven," because our present doesn't yet match God's promise. So we keep striving, praying, moving, pressing, studying, working, attending church, leading Bible studies, singing hymns, taking communion, giving alms, and serving in the community. These are some signs that we desire "on earth as it is in heaven." We want God's future now, God's future present. Many have yearned and dreamed of God's future, such that there are all kinds of end-of-the-world predictions throughout history.

Before the end times imaginary predictions of the *Left Behind* book series, or the visions of Harold Camping, there was the year 1806. In that year, a domesticated hen in Leeds, England, appeared to lay eggs inscribed with the message "Christ is coming." Many people reportedly went to see this hen and began to despair of the coming judgment day. However, it was soon discovered that the eggs were not in fact prophetic messages of the future but the work of their owner, who had been writing on the eggs in ink and reinserting them into the poor hen's body. If it was the end of anything, it was the end of that poor hen! And this whole situation also reminds us that everything that is so-called prophetic may be a pathetic lie.

But before hens or Harolds, there is the Revelation of John, literally the "apocalypse" of John. Don't get nervous, I'm not making any predictions. And John's vision, anyway, is much more hopeful and joyful than the usual doomsday predictions we hear. It's much more expansive than the way we usually live or how we think.

"On earth as it is in heaven"—but our present doesn't seem to match God's promise in this vision. "There was a great multitude that no one could count, from every nation, from all tribes and peoples and languages, standing before the throne and before the Lamb, robed in white, with palm branches in their hands." The palms are signs of joy and triumph. But even in what is considered to be utopia, the perfect world, God's world, God's eternal home, there's a question that arises from this encounter with difference and diversity—from every nation, from all tribes and peoples and languages. And the question is, "Who are these, robed in white, and where have they come from?" Where have *they* come from? Here's someone who already knew the answer to his question, showing us that sometimes we ask questions for which we already know the answer. Do I have to pay my electricity bill this month? Do I really need to get out of bed this morning and go to work? As pastor, do I really need to go to the worship committee meeting where we talked about the last committee meeting where we talked about the last committee meeting? Should I pray? Should I vote? Where have they come from? The elder who asked knew that "These are they who have come out of the great ordeal." He's referring to the persecution of Christians in Asia Minor. A time of brutality under Roman imperialism, which is why Revelation is known as crisis literature. These, in Revelation, were Christian martyrs, who suffered and died for the faith all across the world.

Where have they come from? It's almost as if he's surprised by who is there. Like ants or spiders sneaking their way into our homes, we wonder where *they* came from. You know how we like to say "they" or "them," which is a way of saying "not us." Not our church, not our denomination, not in our house, not in our social clubs and networks. Not in our graduating class. Not at our workplace or in our neighborhood. Not our race. They. Moving into our neighborhoods so we quickly put up a "For Sale" sign to take flight. They. Speaking a language that isn't English and taking employment opportunities "away" from others. They. The way they dress. The way they practice their religion. The way they discuss their gender. They. Where have they come from? We, not they, may be in for the surprise of our lives when we see who is in that great multitude no one can count—from every nation, and all tribes and peoples, and languages. They may not be in our relationship circles but they have always been a part of the circle of God—they came from God, born of God, breathed into this world by God's love. God is not the problem—look at this vision of God's future from John. No, we are the problem.

French philosopher Jacques Derrida and others are on to something when they attempt to deconstruct our binary oppositions. We love binaries.

We adore either/or. White or black. Male or female. Rich or poor. Republican or Democrat. Faith or science. Them or us. And if you live in North Carolina, Eastern Carolina barbeque or Western Carolina barbeque. Duke blue or Tar Heel blue. The binary pits one thing against another with one being greater or better or more powerful. We function with an either/or mentality many times even when it comes to the kingdom of God. Evangelical or mainline. Tongue-talking or wine-tasting Christian. But it's God's kingdom, not ours. Where have they come from? They aren't supposed to be here. They don't have the right ID and not even a GED and they always wear a hoodie. I never met them and God never asked me for a reference letter on their behalf. Where have they come from?

When our operative theological modality is "they" we can quickly *other* someone and stick them in the object camp of nonhuman entity in order to control them. We adore the "or" but God is an "and" God with a wide tent, the great multitude that no one could count. Not you or you, but you and you. Our disjunctive or disjointed vision is why sometimes people don't know if we believe in justice or "just us." But just as suffering is nondiscriminatory for this great number from every nation, from all tribes and peoples, and languages, so is God's love, which will wipe every tear from every eye.

We may be an "or" people, but God is a conjunctive God with a conjunctive imagination. "From every nation, from all tribes and peoples and languages." With the talk about building walls and the treatment of immigrants and refugees ("they") and taking America back from "them," it's so critical to remember God so loved the world, not just the United States of America, because God has a conjunctive imagination. Every nation, from all tribes and peoples and languages. And. This is not a vision of singularity but one of plurality. Not a "me" perspective but a "we" one.

In 2014, *Duke Magazine* did a special cover story on "The Changing Face of Duke." It focused on the growing and largest minority group on Duke's campus—the Asian and Asian American student population with all of their various ethnic identities. Some come from families who lived in the US for years; others are international students. As the article says, this blooming presence on campus is creating a "ripple effect of institutional change along social, cultural, and academic lines."[1] But what was so telling were some of the alumni responses to this cover story through such statements as "Duke's not for me anymore." Me or we?

When Jesus enters the temple in the Gospel of Mark, he reclaims that space as a house of prayer for all nations (Mark 11:17). The day of Pentecost in Acts is a vision of the joining together of many languages and cultures

1. Booher, "Changing Face of Duke."

and ethnicities (Acts 2); it's a Pentecostal surplus of God. Even God, in God's own being, is conjunctive—Father and Son and Holy Spirit, three persons in one. Our future as the people of God is to see the promise to Abraham fulfilled that by his offspring "all the nations of the earth [will] gain blessing for themselves" (Gen 22:17–18). It may take a while for God's promises to be fulfilled but they will be fulfilled. The "and" will come to pass. Both/and, not either/or. Every nation and all tribes and peoples and languages.

> He's got the whole world in His hands
> He's got the whole world in His hands
> He's got the whole world in His hands
> He's got the whole world in His hands
>
> He's got you and me sister in His hands
> He's got you and me sister in His hands
> He's got you and me sister in His hands
> He's got the whole world in his hands.

You *and* me. Conjunctive. God makes room for every nation, from all tribes and peoples and languages. There's always room for more in God's economy. The unknown black bards from the bosom of black slave religion embodied "the more" because, as scholars remind us, slave Christianity was distinct from slaveholding Christianity in that it was nonracist.

> Get on board, little children
> Get on board, little children
> Get on board, little children
> There's room for many-a-more.
>
> The fare is cheap
> And all can go.
> The rich and poor are there
> No second class upon this train
> No difference in the fare.

There's room for many-a-more. There's room for the conjunctive "and." Rich *and* poor.

A choir is not a soloist though some diva sopranos may think they are the choir. For a choir to be a choir we need "and." Sopranos and altos and tenors and basses. Both/and, not either/or. Where have they come from? When we worship at the altar of binary oppositions, even as Christians, we can write people out of the book of humanity, living our disjointed vision rather than the conjunctive hope of God.

A conjunctive imagination recognizes that there is a number in the throne room of God, which no one can number. To function with a conjunction theology is to openly embrace the other; it is anti-closure and anti-dominance. It is the embrace of the wide community of God and the "one great fellowship of love throughout the whole wide earth." We get into trouble when we want to close people out, box them in, shut them up because they don't look like us, act like us, think like us. Just because they are not like us, we think they are not God's. But John's revelation of God's future reminds us that there's a great multitude that no one could count. From east and west, north and south, meeting for fellowship in Christ. The holy rollers and the frozen chosen.

Conjunctions remind us that "If you want to go fast, go alone; [but] if you want to go far [into the future of God], go together." Jimmy Durante was one of the great entertainers in the twentieth century. He was asked to be a part of a show for World War II veterans. He told them his schedule was very busy so he could afford only a few minutes and do one short monologue and then immediately leave for his next appointment. The show's director agreed and was happy that he was coming even with his busy schedule. When Jimmy got on stage, something interesting happened. He performed his short monologue but then he stayed. The applause grew louder and louder and he kept staying. Fifteen, twenty, then thirty minutes went by. Finally, he took his last bow and left the stage. Someone backstage stopped him and said, "I thought you had to go after a few minutes. What happened?" Jimmy answered, "I did have to go, but I can show you the reason I stayed. You can see for yourself if you'll look down on the front row." He pointed to the front row and in the front row were two men, each of whom had lost an arm in the war. One had lost his right arm and the other had lost his left. But together, they were able to clap, and that's exactly what they were doing, loudly and cheerfully. Left and right. Together, they were able to clap. The conjunction allowed them to function.

Together, they were cheerful and made a team. Together, they didn't focus on what they lost but focused on what they had. Together, they were able to do something that they could never do apart. Together, they embodied the coming conjunction of God, which is why the spiritual says, "walk together children and don't get weary."

We may prefer a monochrome past or present, but we have a polychromatic future—ready or not, we will be together. But the question is, will we make room in our hearts and lives for God's "and"—from every nation, from all tribes and peoples and languages? This is not about the collapse of the world but the collapse of myopic stereotypical thinking about others and the kingdom of God, while building up a deeper Christian understanding of life in the conjunctive Jesus Christ who is both divine and human.

It's always been about conjunctions for God, from the very beginning when God created the heavens and the earth. There was an evening and there was a morning. Waters and sky. Plants and trees. Birds and sea creatures. Male and female. God functions with conjunctions—winter and spring and summer and fall. Jews and Gentiles. There are no built walls in the kingdom of God because those walls are torn down in Christ (Eph 2). In Christ, we come together. Immigrants and refugees and orphans and widows and blacks and whites and Latinos and Asians and Native Americans and Parthians and Medes and Elamites and residents of Mesopotamia and Judea and Cappadocia and Pontus and Asia and Phrygia and Pamphylia and Egypt and the parts of Libya belonging to Cyrene, and visitors from Rome, both Jews and proselytes, Cretans and Arabs. Baptists and Episcopalians and Presbyterians and Lutherans and Methodists and Catholics and Nazarenes and Church of God (Anderson) and Church of God (Cleveland) and Church of God in Christ and interdenominational and nondenominational and Peter and James and John and Moses and Elijah and Sonny and Cher and Simon and Garfunkel and Donnie and Marie and Bach and Beyoncé and Batman and Robin and Starsky and Hutch and Popeye and Olive Oil and Tom and Jerry and Phineas and Ferb. And. And. And. And. Every nation, all tribes, all peoples and languages. All are citizens in God's city. Together.

We may want to build walls, but God will eventually just tear them down and finally we'll understand it better by and by. Finally, we'll see the consummation of the holy conjunction when we gather with the angels and elders and the four living creatures and the mosaic multitude from every nation, from all tribes and peoples and languages, crying out to the one seated on the throne and to the Lamb with a conjunctive celebration of never-ending praise, "Blessing and glory and wisdom and thanksgiving and honor and power and might be to our God forever and ever!" Thank God, for the "and."

Questions about the Question

- How do we nurture a conjunctive imagination?
- Why do we often operate in binary thinking?
- Where is the "and" in your life and work?

Postlude

The Bible, Questions, and Worship

The reflections in this book organized around the overarching questions of "Who Is God?," "Who am I?," and "What Should We Do?" have foregrounded questioning as a faithful practice of discipleship, because an interrogative spirituality is often neglected in the life of faith while having answers is usually praised and highlighted. But the Bible reveals that God questions and humans question. The Bible is a question book, and the truth is if we don't have questions, implicitly we are saying that we are God and reveal a level of spiritual hubris rather than humility. Questions are honest because life is so often lived in unresolved, uncertain, and unknown situations. Furthermore, questions lead us to dig deeper and can lead us to learn more about God and come to know God more. We can find God in the questions. How appropriate this is when we follow a God who questions! Questions are faithful witness to the gospel of Jesus Christ and even embody faithful worship of God. They witness and as they do, they can also be worship.

Worship isn't tainted by questions but can be bolstered and broadened by them. *Theologically*, when Dale Andrews, whom I mentioned earlier, repeated his mantra—"I have more questions than answers, more problems than solutions. For this, I give God praise"—he offered insight into the praise of God. With more questions and problems than answers and solutions, he still praises God, which suggests that the praise of God is not based on our circumstances, whether positive or negative. Praise is offered to God because God is God and God is worthy of praise. But questions are an aspect of our praise to God. They are not in opposition to praise because our questions are posed to God and through them, we turn to God, and by turning to God, we glorify God and praise God. A question can call upon God and this might be named "epicletic doxology."[1] In worship, we offer

1. See Old, *Themes and Variations for a Christian Doxology.*

our whole selves, complications, complexes, craziness, concerns, questions, problems, pain, sorrow, joys, hopes and dreams. In other words, we come at "full stretch" before God.[2] Our questions aid us in being at full stretch, with nothing to hide in God's presence. We bring our laments, disbelief, curiosity, and uncertainty to God as an act of worship. We may have more questions than answers, but we still praise.

Questions are not only theologically permissible and admirable but as this book has demonstrated by focusing on questions from the Bible, they are also *biblical*, literally. When worship leaders talk about their desire to have "biblical" worship, nurturing questions is one way to do so. As I've shown, there are divine and human questions ringing out of the Bible and if the Bible as Scripture is the church's book and liturgical guide, it should lead us in the worship practice of lifting queries of various kinds. An obvious link and place to start are the Psalms that raise so many questions of lament: How long, O Lord? Why do the nations conspire and the peoples plot in vain? Why are you downcast, O my soul? Whom shall I fear? The list of questions in the Psalms are amazingly present in the Bible, yet not often present in corporate worship services. The truth is that questions don't have to be lament-full. Maybe they are just wonderings—Will the dust praise you? Will it tell of your faithfulness? (Psalm 30:9) To be so-called biblical in our worship as the people of God means to bring our questions forward and give them voice, regardless of their nature. Perhaps this book is an opportunity to lean into the open nature of questions for Christian worship that seeks to engage the Scriptures in meaningful and fresh ways.

One way toward liturgical freshness is utilizing biblical questions to shape a call to worship for a service. In the following example, I draw on God's questions in Job 38 to create a call to worship:

> **Leader:** Where were you when I laid the foundation of the earth? Who determined its measurements? Who stretched the line upon it? Who laid its cornerstone when the morning stars sang together and all the heavenly beings shouted for joy?
>
> **Congregation:** You, O Lord, we praise.
>
> **Leader:** Who shut in the sea with doors when it burst out from the womb, when I made the clouds its garment and thick darkness its swaddling band, and prescribed bounds for it, and set bars and doors?

2. As noted earlier, this is a term of liturgical theologian Don Saliers. See Anderson and Morill, eds., *Liturgy and the Moral Self.*

Congregation: You, O Lord, we praise.

Leader: Have you commanded the morning since your days began and caused the dawn to know its place? Have you entered into the springs of the sea or walked in the recesses of the deep? Have you comprehended the expanse of the earth?

Congregation: You, O Lord, we praise.

Leader: Have you entered the storehouses of the snow, or have you seen the storehouses of the hail? What is the way to the place where the light is distributed or where the east wind is scattered upon the earth? Who has cut a channel for the torrents of rain and a way for the thunderbolt, to bring rain on a land where no one lives, on the desert, which is empty of human life, to satisfy the waste and desolate land, and to make the ground put forth grass?

Congregation: You, O Lord, we praise.

Leader: From whose womb did the ice come forth, and who has given birth to the hoarfrost of heaven? Who has put wisdom in the inward parts or given understanding to the mind? Who has the wisdom to number the clouds? Or who can tilt the waterskins of the heavens when the dust runs into a mass and the clods cling together?

Congregation: You, O Lord, we praise.

All: Let us worship God.

In addition, if we are honest as church leaders and laity, questions are the backdrop for the planning of worship services. Questions are the background of public *liturgical* expression as well. This is not surprising if we consider that the traditional ordo of the public liturgy is rooted in Luke 24:13ff, where there is the gathering, word, meal, and scattering. In that same post-resurrection scene, when two people are depressed because they believe Jesus is dead, they ask Jesus whom they didn't yet recognize, "Are you the only stranger in Jerusalem who does not know the things that have taken place there in these days?" There are other questions as well in this narrative that is the foundation for the liturgical ordo. One might then say that questions are built into the very nature of the liturgical ordo and thus questions (in)form the public liturgy.

When engaging in worship planning with a team of ministers and musicians, there are many decisions to be made that stem from questions raised. What lectionary texts will be the focus for this Sunday? What is the sermonic focus of the preacher? What songs or hymns are fitting with the liturgical and biblical themes of the day? What liturgical colors should be used? How might we alter the order of service this week in light of the liturgical day or sermon direction? Should we use wine or juice for communion? Is gluten-free bread available? Will we process this week? Will we include a choral benediction or choral introit? All of these questions and many more feed into the liturgy and help shape it. Therefore, questions of all kinds, even practical ones in worship planning, surround the communal worship of the church. These logistical questions are important, but worship planners should also be mindful of the larger existential questions on the hearts and minds of the congregation and explore how to give voice in worship to those real-life questions percolating within the people—Why? How? When? Where? Who? What? If we are attuned to human reality beyond the necessary logistical queries, we will realize even more that questions form the liturgy and are in the liturgy. This is as it should be, as we continue to learn and grow as worship leaders. Raise and listen to the questions because this might be where we find God.

This is good news because many of the people we serve, including ourselves, live the questions, even if they don't love them. To know that God might be found in the question or God asks questions can be very comforting in that we are not alone in our questioning. Embracing this approach to faith and its inclusion in worship leadership and planning is highly *pastoral*. Worship is for and to God; it is theological. But by its very nature, it is also sociological and anthropological. With this perspective, one may see the creation of the space of questioning in worship as an aspect of worship as pastoral care. There's a level of human honesty by their inclusion and there is a path to ministering to the congregation, which includes people with many questions on their hearts and minds. Worship can be a venue for offering those questions and listening to those questions. It could be an open oasis for those queries to flow in and out of song, prayer, or sermon. It is also true that congregants aren't the only ones in a local church with questions; pastors and other leaders have them too! For pastors to acknowledge that they, too, have open-ended questions that are unresolved might be a form of self-pastoral care and an act of liberation not only for them but for others. If only answers to our questions are presented as the way of faith, this could lead some to think they lack faith or are not loved by God or are unbiblical. I hope this book demonstrates that this is far from the truth.

Attentive and sensitive pastors and worship leaders should be able to facilitate and lead the prayers of the people as only questions at some moments and not statements or answers. For instance, the following is one potential approach to the prayers of the people:

> Today, God, we don't come with answers. We come with all of our questions, knowing that in Christ even you ask us questions like "What do you want me to do for you?" You are caring, kind, and gracious. What do we want you to do for us? Look beyond our faults and see our need because at times, we aren't sure if you're paying attention. "Why do we fast [sometimes], but you do not see?" We are not sure what you see, when you see, or if you see.
>
> We see the world and ask like Jeremiah, "Is there no balm in Gilead?"
>
> We see the nation and ponder like Isaiah, "When we expected it to yield grapes, why did it yield wild grapes?"
>
> We see our state and are at a loss for words and wonder, "What shall I cry?"
>
> We gaze upon our city and ponder like Mary, "How can this be?"
>
> We don't have answers. We are burdened with tons of questions. We lift them up today on the way. On our spiritual quest, we embrace the ambiguity of faith and the honesty of all of our questions rising from our hearts. Our questions are still a caress of you.
>
> We still trust through our queries and interrogations because in the cracks of faith we still ask, "Who will separate us from the love of Christ?" We ask that question as an answer, for nothing will separate us from your love.
>
> Let us embrace you through the questions and be still at home.
>
> We don't come with answers, O God. We come with all of our questions, knowing that we find you there. We find you here. On this quest in your presence, we, therefore, ask, "What should we do?" What? Help us to do. Amen.

This prayer could model an interrogative spirituality. Also, a congregation could be asked to write their questions down on a piece of paper as a form of prayer and then those prayers collected and placed in a visible location as part of the worship service. There could be hymns, songs, and choral anthems sung, that raise questions in them, such as "What language shall

I borrow . . . ?"[3] There are diverse ways to engage questions, all the while reassuring the people that their questions are normal and faithful. This is fundamentally a pastoral task.

These four considerations—theological, biblical, liturgical, and pastoral—suggest the importance of the faithful practice of questioning for the church's life of worship. These four are not exhaustive and others could be named but hopefully, these gesture toward some key factors that may energize worship leaders and pastors in fostering creative spaces in congregational life for honest questions to be raised. The Bible is full of questions. God raises questions. We have our own questions on the Way. This is also what it means to be a faithful disciple of Jesus. Live the questions even when you don't love them because in the query is where you might find the Holy.

3. Gerhardt and Alexander, "O Sacred Head, Now Wounded."

Bibliography

Achebe, Chinua. *Things Fall Apart*. New York: Penguin, 1994.

"America's Changing Religious Landscape." *Pew Research Center*, May 12, 2015. https://www.pewforum.org/2015/05/12/americas-changing-religious-landscape/.

Anderson, E. Byron, and Bruce Morill, eds. *Liturgy and the Moral Self: Humanity at Full Stretch Before God—Essays in Honor of Don Saliers*. Pueblo, CO: Liturgical, 1998.

Androzzo, Alma Bazel. "If I Can Help Somebody." 1945. *Find A Grave*. https://www.findagrave.com/memorial/126141617/alma-irene-androzzo_thompson.

Anglund, Joan Walsh. *A Cup of Sun: A Book of Poems*. Boston: Harcourt, 1967.

"Are You God's Wife?" *Stories for Preaching*. https://storiesforpreaching.com.au/sermonillustrations/love-2/are-you-gods-wife/.

Augustine (Saint). "Book IV." In *On Christian Teaching*, translated by R. P. H. Green, 101–46. Orig. 397. Oxford: Oxford University Press, 1997.

———."Book IX.12." In *Confessions*, translated by R. S. Pine-Coffin, 200–203. London: Penguin, 1961.

———. "Book VIII.12." In *Confessions*, translated by R. S. Pine-Coffin, 177–78. London: Penguin, 1961.

Baldwin, James. *The Fire Next Time*. New York: Penguin, 1964.

Barnes, M. Craig. "Savior at Large: John 20:1–18." *The Christian Century*, March 13, 2002. https://www.christiancentury.org/article/2002-03/savior-large.

BBC News. "Born above the floodwaters." March 2, 2000. http://news.bbc.co.uk/2/hi/africa/662472.stm.

Beker, J. Christiaan. *Paul the Apostle: The Triumph of God in Life and Thought*. Philadelphia: Fortress, 1984.

"The Blessing of Unanswered Prayers." *beliefnet*. https://www.beliefnet.com/prayers/protestant/gratitude/the-blessing-of-unanswered-prayers.aspx.

Blount, Brian K. *Can I Get A Witness? Reading Revelation Through African American Culture*. Louisville: Westminster John Knox, 2005.

Blount, Brian K., and Gary W. Charles. *Preaching Mark in Two Voices*. Louisville: Westminster John Knox, 2002.

Boggs, Kelly. "FIRST-PERSON: The power of one courageous person." *Baptist Press*. August 28, 2009. https://www.baptistpress.com/resource-library/news/first-person-the-power-of-one-courageous-person/.

Bonhoeffer, Dietrich. "Ambassadors for Christ." In *The Collected Sermons of Dietrich Bonhoeffer*, edited by Isabel Best, 87–94. Minneapolis: Fortress, 2012.

Booher, Bridget. "The Changing Face of Duke." *Duke Magazine*, February 11, 2014. https://alumni.duke.edu/magazine/articles/changing-face-duke.

Brueggemann, Walter. *An Introduction to the Old Testament: The Canon and Christian Imagination*. Louisville: Westminster John Knox, 2003.

———. *The Psalms and the Life of Faith*. Minneapolis: Fortress, 2004.

Calvin, John. *Institutes of the Christian Religion*, Book III.XX.1. 1845. https://ccel.org/ccel/calvin/prayer/prayer.i.html.

Craddock, Fred. *As One Without Authority*. St. Louis: Chalice, 2001.

———. *Luke*. Interpretation, A Bible Commentary for Teaching and Preaching. Louisville: Westminster John Knox, 1990.

Crouch, Andrae. "Through It All." *YouTube*. https://www.youtube.com/watch?v=CvIxwc90BEI.

"The Curious Case of the Evolving Apostrophe." *MIT Technology Review*, February 4, 2010. https://www.technologyreview.com/2010/02/04/206323/the-curious-case-of-the-evolving-apostrophe/ .

Detweiler, Craig. *iGods: How Technology Shapes our Spiritual and Social Lives*. Grand Rapids: Brazos, 2013.

Dickinson, Emily. "Hope is the thing with feathers." *Poetry Foundation*. https://www.poetryfoundation.org/poems/42889/hope-is-the-thing-with-feathers-314.

Donne, John. "A Valediction of Weeping." *Poetry Foundation*. https://www.poetryfoundation.org/poems/44132/a-valediction-of-weeping#:~:text=PregnantPregnant%20Also%20meaning%3A%20filled,diverse%20shore%20On%20different%20lands.

Dunn, James D. G. *The Theology of Paul the Apostle*. Grand Rapids: Eerdmans, 2006.

Elliott, Charlotte. "Just As I Am." In *African American Heritage Hymnal*, #344. Chicago: GIA, 2001.

Forbes, James. *The Holy Spirit and Preaching*. Nashville: Abingdon, 1989.

Gaither, Gloria, and William J. Gaither. "Because He Lives." In *African American Heritage Hymnal*, #281. Chicago: GIA, 2001.

Gerhardt, Paul, and James Alexander. "O Sacred Head, Now Wounded." In *The United Methodist Hymnal*, #286. Nashville: The United Methodist Publishing House, 1989.

Gomes, Peter J. *The Scandalous Gospel of Jesus: What's So Good about the Good News?* New York: HarperOne, 2007.

"Goodbye Mum." *southernlandlogus.blogspot.com*. https://southernlandlogus.blogspot.com/p/humour.html.

Hart, David Bentley. *The Doors of the Sea: Where Was God in the Tsunami?* Grand Rapids: Eerdmans, 2011.

Hoezee, Scott. *Actuality: Real Life Stories for Sermons That Matter*. Nashville: Abingdon, 2014.

Hughes, Langston. "Mother to Son." *Poetry Foundation*. https://www.poetryfoundation.org/poems/47559/mother-to-son.

Johnson, James Weldon. *God's Trombones: Seven Negro Sermons in Verse*. New York: Viking, 1927.

———. "Lift Every Voice and Sing." In *African American Heritage Hymnal*, #540. Chicago: GIA, 2001.

———. “O Black and Unknown Bards.” 1922. *Poets.org*. https://poets.org/poem/o-black-and-unknown-bards.

Jonas Salk Quotes. https://quote.org/quote/what-people-think-of-as-the-moment-582877.

Julian of Norwich. *Revelations of Divine Love*. Translated by Barry A. Windeatt. Orig. 1670. Oxford: Oxford University Press, 2015.

King, Martin Luther, Jr. “The Drum Major Instinct.” In *A Testament of Hope: The Essential Writings and Speeches of Martin Luther King, Jr.*, edited by James M. Washington, 259–67. San Francisco: HarperSanFrancisco, 1986.

———. “The Three Dimensions of a Complete Life.” Stanford University, The Martin Luther King, Jr. Research and Education Institute, April 9, 1967. https://kinginstitute.stanford.edu/king-papers/publications/knock-midnight-inspiration-great-sermons-reverend-martin-luther-king-jr-6.

Lamott, Anne. *Help, Thanks, Wow: The Three Essential Prayers*. New York: Riverhead, 2012.

Lathrop, Gordon. *Holy Things: A Liturgical Theology*. Minneapolis: Fortress, 1993.

Lazarus, Emma. “The New Colossus.” *poets.org*. https://poets.org/poem/new-colossus?gclid=CjwKCAjw8cCGBhB6EiwAgORey3Ei7sp8XH5fZSDntoUYxEcSmU1J7NwAhWsokclnwlY59zJgvrVTVxoCFmIQAvD_BwE.

Lewis, C. S. *A Grief Observed*. New York: HarperCollins, 2001.

Morrison, Toni. “The Site of Memory.” In *The Source of Self-Regard: Selected Essays, Speeches, and Meditations*, 345–64. New York: Vintage International, 2019.

Murphy, Jack. “Afterlife is a prime subject for humor.” *The Ledger*, October 11, 2009. https://www.theledger.com/news/20091011/afterlife-is-a-prime-subject-for-humor/1.

Murray, Pauli. “Pauli Murray reads ‘Dark Testament.’” *Harvard Radcliffe Institute*. https://www.radcliffe.harvard.edu/news-and-ideas/pauli-murray-reads-dark-testament.

National Endowment for the Humanities. “Conversation with B. B. King.” https://www.neh.gov/humanities/1999/mayjune/conversation/b-b-king-the-blues/.

NORC at the University of Chicago. “National Congregations Study.” https://www.norc.org/Research/Projects/Pages/national-congregations-study.aspx.

Old, Hughes Oliphant. *Themes and Variations for a Christian Doxology: Some Thoughts on a Theology of Worship*. Grand Rapids: Eerdmans, 1992.

Orloff, Judith. “The Health Benefit of Tears.” https://www.psychologytoday.com/us/blog/emotional-freedom/201007/the-health-benefit-tears.

Painter, Nell Irvin. *Sojourner Truth: A Life, A Symbol*. New York: W. W. Norton & Company, 1996.

Palmer, Ray. “My Faith Looks Up To Thee.” In *African American Heritage Hymnal*, #456. Chicago: GIA, 2001.

“The Pan.” *Stories for Preaching*. https://storiesforpreaching.com.au/sermonillustrations/the-pan/.

Podrazik, Joan. “Oprah’s Life Lesson From Maya Angelou: ‘When People Show You Who They Are, Believe Them’ (VIDEO).” *HuffPost*, March 14, 2013. https://www.huffpost.com/entry/oprah-life-lesson-maya-angelou_n_2869235.

Reid, Stephen Breck. *Listening In: A Multicultural Reading of the Psalms*. Nashville: Abingdon, 1997.

Ricoeur, Paul. "The Hermeneutics of Testimony." *Essays on Biblical Interpretation, Religion Online*. https://www.religion-online.org/book-chapter/chapter-3-the-hermeneutics-of-testimony/.

Rilke, Rainer Maria. *Letters to a Young Poet*. https://www.columbia.edu/~ey2172/rilke.html.

Scharen, Christian. *Faith as a Way of Life: A Vision for Pastoral Leadership*. Grand Rapids: Eerdmans, 2008.

Seuss, Dr. *I Can Read With My Eyes Shut*. New York: Penguin Random House, 2013.

Smith, J. Alfred. "Foundations of Our Faith." In *Power in the Pulpit: How America's Most Effective Black Preachers Prepare Their Sermons*, edited by Cleophus J. LaRue, 141–45. Louisville: Westminster John Knox, 2002.

Smith, Luther E. "Conclusion: Embracing the Quest." In *Anchored in the Current: Discovering Howard Thurman as Educator, Activist, Guide, and Prophet*, edited by Gregory C. Ellison II, 165–76. Louisville: Westminster John Knox, 2020.

Spinks, Bryan. *The Worship Mall: Contemporary Responses to Contemporary Culture*. London: SPCK, 2010.

Thurman, Howard. *Jesus and the Disinherited*. Boston: Beacon, 1996.

———. *Meditations of the Heart*. Boston: Beacon, 1999.

Tillet, Salamishah. *Sites of Slavery: Citizenship and Racial Democracy in the Post-Civil Rights Imagination*. Durham, NC: Duke University Press, 2012.

Troeger, Thomas. *Wonder Reborn: Creating Sermons on Hymns, Music, and Poetry*. New York: Oxford University Press, 2010.

van Harn, Roger. *The Lectionary Commentary: Theological Exegesis for Sunday's Texts, the First Readings: The Old Testament and Acts*. Grand Rapids: Eerdmans, 2005.

Washington, Denzel. *Goodreads Quotes*. https://www.goodreads.com/quotes/4108438-you-pray-for-rain-you-gotta-deal-with-the-mud.

Welker, Michael. *God the Spirit*. Minneapolis: Fortress, 1994.

White, James. *The Sacraments in Protestant Practice and Faith*. Nashville: Abingdon, 1999.

Wilson, Paul Scott. *Setting Words on Fire: Putting God at the Center of the Sermon*. Nashville: Abingdon, 2008.

Wolterstorff, Nicholas. *Lament for a Son*. Grand Rapids: Eerdmans, 1987.

Printed in the USA
CPSIA information can be obtained
at www.ICGtesting.com
LVHW091936150923
758309LV00004B/251